Evaluating Commercial BANK PERFORMANCE

A Guide to Financial Analysis

Donald R. Fraser, Ph.D.
Professor of Finance
Texas A&M University
College Station, Texas

and

Lyn M. Fraser, C.P.A.
Lyn Fraser and Associates
Financial Information Services
College Station, Texas

Bankers Publishing Company
Rolling Meadows, Illinois

This publication is designed to provide accurate and authoritative information regarding its subject matter. It is sold with the understanding that the publisher is not engaged in rendering legal, accounting, or other professional service. If legal or other expert assistance is required, the services of a competent professional person should be sought

For Eleanor, Little Bit, and Chester

Contents

List of Figures

List of Tables

Preface

Evaluating Commercial Bank Performance provides a comprehensive set of tools for anyone interested in assessing the financial condition and operating performance of a commercial bank: currently, over time, and in relation to its peers. The well-publicized collapse of numerous banking organizations and the difficulties encountered by many large and small banks underscore the topic's importance.

Much of *Evaluating* is involved with the presentation and analysis of financial statements provided by banks to their shareholders, creditors, and bank regulatory agencies. The focus is, however, much broader in scope since the book encompasses a discussion of environmental factors affecting the role of commercial banks in the economy, reasons for widespread commercial bank failures, the context of bank performance in relation to risk and return, and additional sources of information useful in evaluating the condition and performance of a commercial banking organization.

Principal audiences for this book are (1) banking professionals, especially officers who manage day-to-day banking operations; (2) members of bank boards of directors who make key decisions based on the evaluation of an organization's financial condition and performance; 3) educational institutions, including colleges and universities (the text is useful as a supplement in courses dealing with bank-related issues such as financial institutions, bank management, and money and banking), specialized bank training organizations, and in-house bank training programs; (4) customers of commercial banks–especially depositors and investors in bank debt and equity securities–who are concerned with the financial health of their bank; and (5) banking analysts who review bank performance for purposes of acquisition, merger, or investment decisions.

While some of the concepts discussed are quite complex, the treatment of these issues emphasizes clarity of presentation and understandability, with a minimum of mathematical and statistical analysis. A complete set of references to relevant literature on the topics covered in the chapters is included.

Divided into six chapters, the first–Bank Performance: Evidence and Explanation–is introductory in nature and explains the importance of analyzing the financial health and performance of commercial banks from the perspective of bank shareholders, depositors, and other creditors. Shareholders and uninsured depositors (those with accounts of over $100,000; principally businesses) are especially concerned about the funds they have at risk. The chapter also discusses the vital significance of the health of commercial banks to society as a whole. Financial data tracing important recent developments in the performance of commercial banks are presented, as is an exploration of the rising trend and causes of bank failures.

Chapter 2–The Dimensions of Bank Performance– treats the various conceptual dimensions of bank performance, including earnings and risk. While the focus of the chapter is on dimensions of bank performance that can be measured from data provided in the balance sheet and income statements, other aspects of bank performance are also discussed. In addition, this chapter covers the financial and nonfinancial sources of information available to those interested in evaluating bank performance.

Chapters 3, 4, and 5 fit together as a clear subset of the book and center on analyzing bank financial statements. Banks systematically file required financial information with the regulatory authorities, and this information is compiled in a uniform format for all insured commercial banking institutions in the United States. The material is published in a document called *The Uniform Bank Performance Report*, available to banks and the general public on a quarterly and annual basis. With the uniform financial data as background, Chapters 3, 4, and 5 show users how to access bank financial statements for the purpose of evaluating the organization's financial condition and performance.

Chapter 3–Presentation of Bank Financial Statements: Balance Sheet and Income Statements–covers the organization of bank financial statements as a beginning step in interpreting banking financial data. A step-by-step guide through the components of bank balance sheets and income statements, based on actual bank financial statements, is provided.

Chapter 4–The Tools of Financial Statement Analysis–deals with how the analyst can use this information to assess the performance and condition of a bank. It contains a description of financial ratios and other analytical tools commonly used in interpreting bank financial statements.

Chapter 5–Analysis of Bank Financial Statements–applies these tools of financial analysis to evaluate two actual banks–one a small community bank, the other a large metropolitan bank. A discussion of the quality of financial reporting and how the qualitative dimension impacts financial analysis is also included.

Chapter 6–Predicting Bank Financial Distress and Failure–provides the reader with additional information relevant to the evaluation of bank performance beyond that which is possible through ratio analysis. Evidence from studies that have used stock and bond price data to predict bank performance is also presented.

The authors would like to thank Tanya Dean for her careful, patient typing of this manuscript throughout its many drafts, and for doing so with an ever-cheerful disposition.

We would also like to note an interesting coincidence that emerged in the process of writing this book. One of the financial ratios used to evaluate bank risk is identical to our daughter Eleanor's favorite clothing store: The GAP. We hope our readers will provide insight as to how we should interpret this information.

Donald R. Fraser
Lyn M. Fraser

February, 1990
College Station, Texas

1

Bank Performance: Evidence and Explanation

Bank performance is important to a number of different audiences for a variety of reasons. In a private enterprise economy in which commercial banks are privately owned (as in the United States and most developed countries), the financial performance of banks is obviously of great concern to their shareholders. The ability of commercial banks to provide a reasonable return to their owners in the form of cash dividends or other means of compensation depends upon their ability to earn a reasonable return on assets without assuming excessive risk.

A commercial bank's financial performance is also of great significance to depositors and other creditors. The ability of commercial banks to meet the withdrawal needs of depositor and nondepositor customers is ultimately dependent upon the risk/return characteristics of bank portfolios. While the existence of deposit insurance for domestic deposits up to $100,000 (as of late 1990) does insulate depositors to a degree from the financial consequences of inadequate bank performance, large depositors must still be concerned about the risk of losing their deposits. A number of proposals for reform of the deposit insurance systems have incorporated a recommendation for reducing the ceiling level of insured deposits, perhaps lowering the insured amount of deposits from the current $100,000 to a much more modest $10,000.

While the financial performance of commercial banks is important for shareholders, depositors, and other creditors, financial performance (especially in floundering and failing banks) takes on special significance from a social perspective. This significance—and the reason that bank failures are treated differently by governments than the failure of other retailers—stems from the potential for the failure of one bank to cause a failure of the banking system. This contagion or spillover effect of an individual bank failure occurred dramatically in the early 1930s when the banking system collapsed. While the failure of an individual bank is tolerable, the failure of the banking system is intolerable. Concern with the contagion potential of an individual bank failure also produces greater concern (and differential public policy) over large as contrasted to small bank failures. For example, the financial distress at Continental Illinois, one of the ten largest U.S. banking organizations, gave rise to a concerted rescue effort by the Federal Reserve, the Federal Deposit Insurance Corporation (FDIC), and other government agencies, producing a complicated "bail out" for that organization. No such bail out was fashioned for the seventy-nine primarily small banks that failed in 1984—the year of the Continental Illinois rescue.

Concern about the financial health of commercial banks has been heightened by growing signs of instability in the entire financial services sector. Perhaps the most publicized evidence of financial problems was the virtual collapse of the savings and loan industry. By early 1990, it was estimated that the number of insolvent savings and loans might exceed 1,000, and that the cost to the U.S. government to restructure the industry and "bail out" the Federal Savings and Loan

Insurance Corporation might exceed $200 billion. However, financial distress has also surfaced at a number of insurance companies and other types of financial service firms. With the sharp increase in the use of financial leverage at nonfinancial corporations (often associated with leveraged buyouts), many analysts fear that the next economic contraction may force a wave of defaults on loans from banks and others, thereby contributing to even greater distress at financial service organizations.

Trends in Financial Performance

While there are many dimensions to the financial performance of commercial banks, the focus here is on two key aspects: *profitability* and *risk*. The financial performance of a commercial banking organization is obviously better if its profits are higher and its risk lower. In practice, high profit generally necessitates accepting greater amounts of risk, and it is one of the principal functions of bank management to balance profit and risk to achieve the goals of the organization.

Profitability. Table 1-1 provides summary data on the profitability of insured commercial banks from 1983–1989. The measure of profitability is the return on assets, calculated by dividing net profit after taxes by the volume of assets.

The data in Table 1-1 illustrate at least three important relationships with respect to bank financial performance. First, commercial banks earn a very low percentage of return on their assets. Historically, a return on assets of one percent after taxes was considered a good one, though few banks have achieved this in recent years. Second, commercial banks experienced erratic and perhaps declining profitability in the 1980s. Third, the relationship between bank size and returns on assets takes a pyramid form, with the highest returns on assets generally in the $100 million–$1 billion range. Extremely large banks, with total assets above $1 billion, usually earn the smallest return on assets.

The small return on assets earned by commercial banks is quite evident from the data in Table 1-1, with insured banks taken as a group never earning, on average, as much as one percent of total assets during the 1983-1989 period. In fact, in 1989, the average return for all commercial banks was less than six-tenths of one percent. As a result, small changes in revenue or costs can produce large changes in the return on assets. Increased competition in the loan market, resulting in reduced loan rates, or increased competition in the deposit market, resulting in increased cost of deposits, will quickly translate into reduced returns on assets.

How can commercial banks attract capital with such a low return on assets? As private, profit-seeking enterprises, banks must offer a competitive risk-adjusted return to the equity market. Clearly, one percent (or less) is insufficient. As discussed throughout this book, banks "lever up" their return on assets to a much higher (and competitive) return on each dollar of equity by using a small amount of equity to finance a large amount of assets. Banks are among the most highly leveraged organizations, a fact that has considerable implications for bank risk-taking and is one of the reasons for the friction that often permeates the relationship between bankers and their regulators.

Not only are returns on assets relatively small for insured commercial banks, but those returns have been unstable. There is some evidence that the return on assets for all insured commercial banks declined during the 1980s. The reduction was especially large for banks with less than $100 million in assets, perhaps reflecting the greater impact of deregulation on smaller banks. For example, the return on assets at banks with total assets of less than $100 million fell from 1.24 percent in 1983 to 0.67 percent in 1988, a decline of almost fifty percent. In contrast, the return on assets for banks with total assets of $100 million to $1 billion fell from 0.93 percent in 1983 to 0.75 percent in 1988, a decline of less than thirty percent.[1]

The relationship between bank profitability and bank size for a given year is also of interest and often seems to take the form of an "irregular" pyramid, with middle-sized banks earning a higher return on assets than the smallest or largest banks. In 1989, for example, banks with total assets of $100 million to $1 billion earned almost one percent on their assets–higher than any of the larger or smaller size groups. This irregular pyramid relationship between bank size and bank profitability may reflect the existence of cost economies for middle-sized banks. Most studies of economies of scale in banking suggest that cost economy advantages, which are never large, disappear at relatively low levels of total assets. These cost economies may allow middle-sized banks to obtain a greater return on assets without generating higher revenues per dollar of assets. The greater returns on assets for middle-sized banks may also reflect the ability of these banks to generate a higher gross revenue per dollar of assets than the other size banks. For example, these middle-sized banks usually operate in a less competitive loan market (and sometimes a less competitive deposit market) than multibillion dollar banks. At the same time, these banks may be large

---

1. It should be recognized that the profitability reports (and hence the return on asset ratio) for the very large, multinational banks are somewhat suspect due to their treatment of the billions of dollars of loans to the less developed countries (LDCs), most of which will probably never be collected.

enough to achieve efficient diversification of risk as compared to the very small-sized banks and thereby translate the higher potential returns into higher actual returns.

Examining changes in the size/return-on-asset relationship over the 1983-1989 period suggests what may be a fundamental change in this relationship, with the maximum return on assets shifting over time to larger banks. In 1983 and 1984, the maximum return on assets occurred at banks with less than $100 million in assets. By 1985, the return on assets for the $100 million to $1 billion size group equaled that of smaller banks, and exceeded that of banks with $1 billion or more in total assets. This shifting relationship may be a temporary phenomenon reflecting the volatility in eco-

Table 1-1
Percentage Return on Assets
For FDIC Insured Commercial Banks

		Asset Size Distribution			
	All Banks	Less than $100 million	$100-1,000 million	$1-10 billion	Greater than $10 billion
1983	0.78	1.24	0.93	0.67	0.54
1984	0.56	1.00	0.94	0.74	-0.02
1985	0.75	0.92	0.91	0.78	0.60
1986	0.60	0.63	0.80	0.80	0.32
1987	0.72	0.72	0.85	0.84	0.55
1988	0.71	0.67	0.75	0.67	0.74
1989*	0.58	0.90	0.94	0.84	0.08

*First Three Quarters, Annual Rate
Source: FDIC

nomic and financial conditions during the 1980s or it may be permanent, reflecting fundamental changes in the competitiveness of small and large banks. (It is important to note that the shifting pattern in profitability at banks of different sizes took place during a period of deposit rate and geographic deregulation and of great changes in technology.) While only additional data over a more extensive time period will settle this issue, the permanence of this trend is obviously of great importance to bankers and the customers they serve.

Risk. There are many dimensions of bank risk encompassing credit, interest rate, liquidity, etc. The net effects of these types of risk should be reflected in the number of banks that fail, become problems, and become subject to increased surveillance by the regulatory authorities. By these standards, it would appear that risk has increased in the banking industry during recent years. For example, Table 1-2 provides the total number of insured commercial banks that failed in each year from 1960 through late 1989. As shown in that Table, the number of bank failures did not reach ten in any year from 1960 through 1974. Bank failures increased in 1975 and 1976 following the 1973-1974 recession but fell back to a lower level in 1977 and 1978. The total number of failures began to rise in the early 1980s and reached 221 in 1988.

Equally important, though not shown in Table 1-2, is the increase in the number of failures at large banks. The failure of a small bank is, of course, significant to its shareholders, depositors, other creditors, employees, and the community it serves (particularly if it is the only supplier of bank services to a small town). However, the failure of a small bank has limited social consequence. Conversely, the failure of a large bank can potentially destabilize the entire financial system. It is therefore not surprising that following the Continental Illinois crisis, the Comptroller of the Currency declared that

Table 1-2
Number of Bank Failures
1960-1989

Year	Number of Failures
1960	2
1961	9
1962	3
1963	2
1964	8
1965	9
1966	8
1967	4
1968	3
1969	9
1970	8
1971	6
1972	3
1973	6
1974	4
1975	14
1976	17
1977	6
1978	7
1979	10
1980	10
1981	10
1982	42
1983	48
1984	78
1985	118
1986	144
1987	201
1988	221
1989 (through September 30)	162

Source: FDIC

the eleven largest U.S. banks were "too big to fail." Financial distress and failure at many large banks in the late 1980s occupied much of the attention of the bank regulatory authorities.

Banks that fail usually have been "problems" prior to the date of failure; indeed, some banks are "problem" banks for a number of years before their failure. (Of course, many banks that become problems correct their shortcomings and return to non-problem status rather than failing.) Table 1-3 provides information on the number of banks on the FDIC's problem bank list for the period 1970 through 1989. As shown in that table, the number of problem banks has increased dramatically, roughly paralleling the growth in bank failures (the number of problem banks may be considered a leading indicator of the number of bank failures). The number of problem banks increased in the mid 1970s, fell in the late 1970s, and then increased dramatically. In fact, the number of problem banks now exceeds 1000, almost 10 percent of all insured banks.

Causes of Recent Bank Failures

Bovenzi and Nejezchleb (of the FDIC) have explored the causes of recent bank failures, emphasizing the significance of recent recessions, problems in particular regions and industries, high real interest rates, and deregulation.[2] They have discovered that general economic conditions such as the unemployment rate play an important role in the higher failure rate.

Other factors such as changes in financial markets and the upsurge in new bank charters also seem to be important. The

---

2. John Bovenzi and Lynn Nejezchleb, "Bank Failures: Why Are There So Many?" *Issues in Bank Regulation.* (Winter 1985): 54–68.

Table 1-3
The Number of Problem Banks
1970-1987

Year	Number of Problem Banks
1970	215
1971	239
1972	190
1973	155
1974	181
1975	347
1976	379
1977	368
1978	342
1979	287
1980	217
1981	220
1982	369
1983	642
1984	848
1985	1,098
1986	1,457
1987	1,559
1988	1,394
1989 (September 30)	1,151

Source: Annual Reports of The Federal Deposit Insurance Corporation, Statistical Abstract of the United States (various issues).

impact of the deregulation of interest rates on the recent failure rate was difficult to ascertain, though the existence of deposit rate deregulation should contribute to an increase in the failure rate in the future.

It is interesting to note that Bovenzi and Nejezchleb projected, based upon their model, that bank failures would average about ten per quarter during the first quarter of 1985. The failure rate was, in fact, more than double that number.

Short, O'Driscoll and Berger (of the Federal Reserve Bank of Dallas) have examined the possibility that bank failures reflect the portfolio decisions made by the asset and liability managers of banks. They compared bank financial performance ratios in 1964, 1975, and 1982-83, with emphasis on the following measures of the risk exposure of U.S. banks: the ratio of loans to assets, the ratio of U.S. Treasury securities to assets, the ratio of other securities to assets, the ratio of capital to assets, the ratio of core deposits to total liabilities, and the ratio of purchased funds to total liabilities. After analyzing a time series of these ratios, they concluded:

> The results of this study indicate that management decisions to incur portfolio risk have played a significant role in the determination of bank failures. The results also suggest that the banking system as a whole is more exposed to risk. (p. 12)[3]

Both of the previous studies dealt with all banks that have failed since the early 1970s, without distinguishing between small and large. In the 1970s the major problem and failed banks were Franklin National, Security National, U.S. National Bank of San Diego, Commonwealth National Bank,

---

3. Eugenia D. Short, Gerald R. O'Driscoll, Jr., and Franklin D. Berger, "Recent Bank Failures: Determinants and Consequences," Paper presented at the 1985 Conference on Bank Structure and Competition, Federal Reserve Bank of Chicago.

and Hamilton National Bank. In the first half of the 1980s, the major problem and failed banks were Continental National, First Pennsylvania, United American Banks, and PennSquare. After analyzing the causes, Sinkey concluded that external economic events were contributing but not determining factors for these problem and failed banks. Fundamentally, it is lack of skill on the part of bank managers that causes bank failures.[4]

One of the most extensive analyses of the causes of bank failures was done by the office of the Comptroller of the Currency.[5] This study focused on three issues: (1) Why do banks develop problems? (2) Why do some banks recover while others fail? and (3) Why do some banks stay healthy? To develop information on these questions, the study analyzed 171 failed banks, fifty-one rehabilitated banks in similar circumstances that experienced significant difficulties but subsequently recovered, and thirty-eight healthy banks that maintained composite CAMEL ratings of 1 or 2 throughout the period of the study. (Under the CAMEL system, individual banks are scored from 1 [best] to 5 [worst] for each of the following criteria: Capital Adequacy, Asset Quality, Management, Earnings, and Liquidity.) Echoing the previous research, the study concluded:

> ...while poor economic conditions make it more difficult for a bank to steer a profitable course, the policies and procedure of a bank's management and board of directors have the greater influence on whether a bank will succeed or fail. In other words,

---

4. Joseph F. Sinkey, Jr., "The Characteristics of Large Problem and Failed Banks," *Issues in Bank Regulation*, (Winter 1985): 42-52.

5. Office of the Comptroller of the Currency, "Bank Failure: An Evaluation of the Factors Contributing to the Failure of National Banks," U.S. Government Printing Office, (Washington, D.C. 1988)

poor management and other internal problems are the common denominator of failed and problem banks. (p. 1)

The following factors appeared to be related to the chances of failure:

1. Nonexistent or poorly followed loan policies (eighty-eight percent of the failed banks)
2. Inadequate systems to ensure compliance with internal policies or banking laws (sixty-nine percent)
3. Inadequate controls or supervision of key bank officers or departments (sixty-two percent)
4. Inadequate problem loan identification systems (fifty-nine percent)
5. Decisions made by one dominant individua –e.g. CEO, Chairman, or principal shareholder (fifty-seven percent) and
6. Nonexistent or poorly followed asset and liability management policies (forty-nine percent)

Insider abuse such as self-dealing, undue dependence on the bank for income or services by a board member or shareholder, inappropriate transactions with affiliates, or unauthorized transactions by management officials, was a significant factor leading to failure in thirty-five percent of the failed banks. Moreover, about one-fourth of the banks with significant insider abuse also had problems involving material fraud which played a notable role in eleven percent of the failures.

The importance of portfolio policies as determined by the management of a bank in affecting the chances of bank failure was indicated in a study at the Federal Reserve Bank of Dallas.[6] In that study, portfolio management strategies

---

6. Jeffery W. Gunther, *Texas Banking Conditions: Managerial Versus Economic Conditions,* Federal Reserve Bank of Dallas, (October 1989)

were used as a proxy for managerial risk taking, and a sample of Texas banks was divided into two groups – aggressively managed and conservatively managed – based upon their portfolios *prior* to the decline in the Texas economy. After examining the financial performance of the banks over time, the study concluded:

> The severe asset-quality problems that emerged at the aggressively managed Texas banks illustrate the financial difficulties that can result from the combination of aggressive banking practices and large swings in economic activity. The financial difficulties of the conservatively managed Texas banks were much less severe, though still substantial. (p. 12)

In fact, as Table 1-4 shows, 7.3 percent of the loans at aggressively managed banks were nonperforming by 1986

Table 1-4
Average Nonperforming Loan Rates,
Medium-Sized Texas Banks, 1986
(Percent)

	Aggressive	Conservative
Total	7.3	4.0
Consumer	1.5	1.5
Commercial and Industrial	6.7	4.2
Real Estate	9.0	4.9

Source: Jeffery W. Gunther, *Texas Banking Conditions: Managerial versus Economic Conditions*, Federal Reserve Bank of Dallas, (October 1989): 7.

while the conservative banks had only 4.0 percent of their loans nonperforming.

A recent study at the Federal Reserve Bank of Philadelphia suggests that size itself may be one of the prime causes of bank failures.[7] The study argues that very small banks, especially those of $25 million or less in total assets, are at such a cost and competitive disadvantage that their survivability is doubtful. Indeed, as shown in Figure 1-1, the failure rate at small banks over the 1984-88 period was much higher than at larger banks.

Figure 1-1
Percentage of Failing Banks by Size
1984–1988

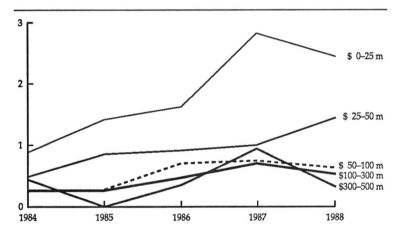

Source: Sherrill Shaffer, "Challenges to Small Banks' Survival," Federal Reserve Bank of Philadelphia, *Business Review*, (September/October 1989): 18.

---

7. Sherrill Shaffer, "Challenges to Small Bank Survival," *Federal Reserve Bank of Philadelphia Business Review*, (September–October 1989): 15–17.

The Cost of Bank Failure

The private cost of bank failure to shareholders, creditors, and occasionally to depositors is substantial. Some information on the dimensions of this loss is provided in Table 1-5, which shows the loss on assets and costs to the FDIC from failures in 1985 and 1986. Loss is divided into those cases in which the FDIC sold the failed bank to another banking organization (referred to as a "Purchase and Assumption") and those cases in which the FDIC liquidated the assets and paid off uninsured depositors, other creditors, and shareholders if (in the unlikely event) there are sufficient assets. Insured depositors in a bank failure are, of course, paid off immediately from the deposit insurance fund.

TABLE 1-5
Estimated Loss on Assets and Cost to FDIC in Bank Failures During 1985 and 1986, by Type of Transaction[1]

	P&As	Payoffs	Difference
Loss on assets	32.0	35.9	(3.9)
Less:			
Book capital	1.5	(0.1)	1.6
Premium	2.1	0.0	2.1
Uninsureds' loss	0.0	0.7	(0.7)
Cost to FDIC	28.4	35.3	(6.9)

[1]All figures are as a percentage of bank assets.

Source: John Bovenzi and Arthur Morton, "Resolution Costs of Bank Failures," *FDIC Banking Review*, Vol. 1, No. 1, (Fall 1988): 8.

As shown in Table 1-5, the FDIC experienced more than a thirty percent loss on assets from the 1985 and 1986 failures– 32.0 percent in purchase and assumption transactions and 35.9 percent in payoff transactions. The difference in cost to the FDIC was even greater than the difference in the loss in assets–28.4 percent cost to the FDIC in purchase and assumptions and 35.3 percent in payoffs. There may be two reasons for this difference. First, the banks handled by payoff may have had poorer quality assets than the banks handled by purchase and assumption which may have reduced bidders for the bank and reduced any potential for outside injection of capital. Second, there may have been differences in the value of the same assets depending upon whether they were disposed of by an ongoing organization or by the FDIC.

Major Factors Affecting Performance

The previous discussion suggests that the decade of the 1980s was marked by declining bank profitability and increased bank risk. What caused these trends? Are they likely to continue? These are important issues for bank analysts to address.

Changes in the performance of commercial banks and other suppliers of financial services appear to reflect the confluence of a number of economic, technological, and regulatory factors (see Figure 1-2). Analysts of bank performance should be aware of the major factors affecting the competitive position of individual banks and include an analysis of these factors when they evaluate bank performance. The principal factors at work, with emphasis on those that have most directly affected commercial banks, are the following:

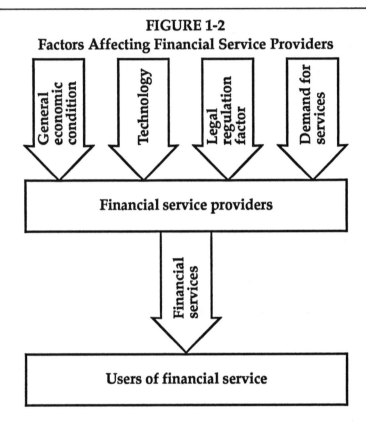

FIGURE 1-2
Factors Affecting Financial Service Providers

Source: U.S. Congress, Office of Technology Assessment, "Effects of Information Technology on Financial Service Providers," (Washington, D.C., 1984): 4.

Inflation and High and Volatile Interest Rates. The inflation rate and interest rates were relatively low and stable through the 1950s and early 1960s. Beginning in 1966, however, the inflation rate began to rise, interest rates increased, and intense pressure was placed on the financial system. The pressure was most severe at the highly regulated commercial banks which (along with other depository institutions) were subject to a regulatory structure designed in the 1930s.

High inflation and high interest rates encouraged other less regulated financial service firms to develop new products such as money market funds and the Cash Management Account–types of products that the traditional intermediaries could not offer due to regulatory constraints.

Advances in Technology have greatly affected the competitive position of different providers of financial services and the ability of financial institutions to compete directly with the capital market in the intermediation function. Rapid advances in electronic technology have lowered costs for processing financial transactions. Those firms which have been most effective in implementing the new financial technology have achieved an edge through lower costs. Advances in technology have made the production of diverse financial services within one firm more feasible by increasing the prospects for realizing economies of scope (which exist when two different products can be produced less expensively at one firm than at two separate firms). Also, advanced financial technology has increased greatly the geographical boundaries over which financial services can be produced, thereby substantially intensifying the extent of competition in the industry.

More sophisticated consumers have also played a major role in the changing structure of the financial services industry. Greater education in personal money management along with high real and nominal returns on financial assets made the flow of funds more volatile. Consumers of financial services increasingly move funds around for very small differences in expected returns.

Securitization, the process of making some or all of the loan portfolio marketable by establishing pools of loans and selling interest (securities in the pools), has also had a substantial impact on the structure of the financial services industry. The process involves the creation of these pools by investment bankers in order to bypass the traditional intermediation process. The phenomenal success of various mortgage pools (most notably the GNMAs) is the most publicized example of securitization. Until early 1986, securitization had been limited to the mortgage markets, especially for government insured and guaranteed mortgages related to residential real estate, and its impact had been more pronounced at thrift institutions than at commercial banks. Recently, however, investment bankers have created pools of consumer and commercial loans. The net result of the securitization of various types of credit is to reduce the market share of commercial banks and other traditional suppliers of funds and to increase the competition for the remaining loans.

Deregulation has also affected the operations of commercial banks and other financial institutions. However, with the exception of the deregulation of commission rates on equity trading in the 1970s, most deregulation has followed changes in market conditions rather than leading the financial system into a new structure. The deregulation of the interest rates that commercial banks and other depository institutions can pay for funds or charge on loans was perhaps the most important aspect of the deregulation phenomenon as it affected commercial banks in the 1980s. The term "Regulation Q" is commonly used to summarize deposit rate limitations while usury laws relate to interest rates charged on loans. Passage of the Depository Institutions Deregulation and Monetary Control Act of 1980 (DIDMCA) and the Garn St-Germain Depository Institutions Act of 1982 set in motion a series of actions that by 1986 had virtually ended all interest rate ceilings at commercial banks and other depository institutions. In contrast, the pace of change in product deregulation (allowing commercial banks to expand their financial services activities beyond their traditional transactions and intermediation services) and geographical deregulation (which principally is the issue of interstate banking) has been much slower.

Geographical deregulation is primarily the result of actions taken by state governments to expand intrastate bank expansion powers and allow interstate banking. Commercial banks and other depository institutions, however, remain enmeshed in a web of regulations that generally limit their operations to one state and sometimes one location within a state.

The severe restrictions on geographical expansion that have traditionally constrained U.S. commercial banks have produced a banking structure quite different from those in most other developed countries where such restrictions generally do not exist. Geographic restrictions have contributed to the exceedingly large number of commercial banks (more than 14,000) in the U.S. as compared to most other countries. As a result, the largest banks in the United States hold a much smaller share of deposits and loans than is the case in most other developed countries.

While the U.S. banking structure remains fragmented compared with those in other industrial countries, the number of U.S. banking organizations has been declining due to mergers, the consolidation of holding company subsidiaries, and failures. As a result, the concentration of banking assets has increased. The largest 100 banking organizations in the U.S., as shown in Table 1-6, increased their share of total bank assets from 50.2 percent in 1977 to 61.5 percent in 1987. This increased concentration was the result of growth at banks that ranked from eleven to 100 as the top ten banking organizations saw their market shares decline slightly.

Table 1-6
Shares of Domestic Banking Assets Accounted For
by the Largest Banking Organizations

Percent

Year	Rank by asset size				
	1-10	11-25	26-50	51-100	Top 100
1987........	20.2	14.6	13.5	13.2	61.5
1986........	20.0	13.5	12.7	12.9	59.1
1985........	20.3	12.8	12.6	12.0	57.7
1984........	20.3	12.8	10.4	11.5	55.0
1983........	21.0	12.8	9.4	54.3	54.3
1982........	21.8	12.4	8.8	10.6	53.6
1981........	21.1	12.0	8.5	10.1	51.7
1980........	21.6	11.5	8.5	9.8	51.4
1979........	21.3	11.3	8.9	9.7	51.2
1978........	21.1	11.3	8.7	9.7	50.8
1977........	21.0	11.0	8.5	9.7	50.2

Source: Dean Amel and Michael Jacowski, "Trends in Banking Structure Since the mid-1970's." *Federal Reserve Bulletin*. (March 1989): 126.

The action by various states to allow interstate banking has been particularly significant. By late 1989, almost all states had passed some form of interstate banking legislation, allowing bank holding companies from other states to acquire banks in those states. It appears increasingly likely that nationwide interstate banking will begin through regional compacts among states rather than through alteration of federal law, reflecting the reluctance of the U.S. Congress to deal with the issue. Table 1-7 provides information on the extent of interstate banking through state initiatives.

Table 1-7 – Broadening the Ability of Banks to Expand Geographically

| | INTRASTATE AND INTERSTATE EXPANSION | | | EXISTING BRANCHING LAWS | | |
| | Intrastate expansion | | | | | |
Decade	Bank branching	Multibank holding companies	Interstate banking	Statewide branching	Limited branching	Unit banking
1970s....	Iowa Maine New Jersey New York Ohio Virginia	Georgia Michigan New York	Maine	Alabama[1] Alaska Arizona California Connecticut Delaware Florida[1] Georgia[1] Hawaii Idaho Indiana[1] Kansas[1] Maine Maryland Massachusetts Michigan Mississippi[1,2] Nebraska[1] Nevada New Hampshire New Jersey New York North Carolina North Dakota[1] Ohio Oklahoma[1] Oregon Rhode Island South Carolina Utah Vermont Virginia Washington	Arkansas[2] Iowa Kentucky Louisiana Minnesota Missouri New Mexico Pennsylvania[2] Tennessee Texas Wisconsin	Colorado Illinois Montana Wyoming
1980s....	Alabama Connecticut Florida Georgia Indiana Kansas Massachusetts Michigan Minnesota Mississippi Nebraska New Hampshire North Dakota Ohio Oklahoma Oregon Pennsylvania Tennessee Texas Utah Washington West Virginia	Arkansas Illinois Indiana Kansas Kentucky Louisiana Nebraska Oklahoma Pennsylvania Washington West Virginia	All except five states[3]			

1. Statewide branching by merger.
2. These states will permit statewide branching in the future: Arkansas in 1999; Mississippi in 1989; and Pennsylvania in 1990.
3. The five are Hawaii, Iowa, Kansas, Montana, and North Dakota.

Source: Dean Amel and Michael Jacowski, "Trends in Banking Structure Since the mid-1970's", *Federal Reserve Bulletin*, (March 1989): 121.

Globalization of the operation of financial service organizations has also affected the operations and structure of these organizations. Funds increasingly flow across national borders for long run investment purposes and short run liquidity management. Reflecting global funds flows, many financial service organizations have expanded globally. Foreign financial service organizations have entered the U.S. market and many U.S. financial service firms have expanded abroad. The net result of this global integration of financial markets is growing competition among financial service firms.

The impact of entry by foreign banks into the U.S. market has been striking in affecting the market penetration of U.S. banks. U.S. banking assets of foreign banks in 1986 exceeded $500 billion, representing nineteen percent of all U.S. banking assets. In terms of total assets, the Japanese banks are dominant, though Canadian, British, and Italian banks also play major roles. Foreign banks now account for approximately twenty percent of all commercial and industrial loans outstanding to U.S. addresses.

New Competitors

One of the most striking changes in the structure of the financial services industry has been the expansion of services by nondepository organizations–those principally financial in nature and especially those (such as retailers and manufacturers) that in past years played only a small part in providing financial services.

The Federal Reserve Bank of New York examined the market shares and profitability of the major competitors to commercial banks in three markets: credit markets, savings markets, and securities markets. It found that, while there had been significant changes in the market shares in many

Table 1-8
Trends in Market Shares of Banks and Nonbanks

Market	Trend in Banks' Share	Banks' Share in 1984	Main Nonbank Competitor
Consumer Lending	Fluctuates	46%	Finance Companies and Thrifts
Automobile Loans	Fluctuates	50	Finance Companies
Revolving Credit	Increasing	60	Retailers
Other[1]	Flat	35	Thrifts
Commercial Lending	Increasing	36	Securities
Mortgage Lending			
Residential[2]	Increasing	27	Thrifts
Commercial	Increasing	36	Life Insurers
Savings Deposits	Flat	46	Thrifts
Individual Retirement Accounts	Declining	28	Thrifts
Discount Stock brokerage	Increasing	55[3]	Securities Firms
Pension Fund Management	Declining	36	Investment Advisors
Underwriting Domestic Issues	Fluctuates	17	Securities Firms
Municipal GO	Declining	27	Securities Firms
Municipal Revenue[4]	Increasing	22	Securities Firms
Private Placements	Fluctuates	9	Securities Firms
Eurodollar Issues	Increasing	27	Foreign Firms
Mergers and Acquisitions	Fluctuates	2	Investment Banks

1. Includes mobile home loans.
2. Includes holdings of mortgage-backed securities.
3. Considering only members of the New York Stock Exchange.
4. Housing and higher education bonds.

Source: "Trends in the Profitability of Commercial Banks," Federal Reserve Bank of New York, (1987).

submarkets, banks are maintaining their traditional shares of the markets open to them. Table 1-8 provides a brief overview of the major financial services offered by commercial banks, their principal competitors, and the trend in the market shares held by commercial banks.

Within the credit markets, bank share of consumer lending has been quite volatile. In fact, bank share of consumer installment credit fell to a low of 42.9 percent in 1982, after remaining at near fifty percent throughout the 1970s. The decline in bank market share reflected the competition from finance companies, particularly the captive finance companies owned by the automobile companies. By 1984, however, the market share of commercial banks had improved, though cut-rate financing in 1986 and 1987 again reduced the market share of commercial banks. Declines in bank market share due to a loss of automobile financing have, however, been offset by the growth of bank-sponsored credit cards. Banks had nearly a sixty percent share of revolving credit at year-end 1984, as compared to forty-seven percent in 1977.

The commercial bank share of the business loan market has been relatively stable, with a slight upward trend. Excluding commercial mortgage loans, commercial bank lending to business (as a share of the total market) appears to have remained almost unchanged from 1970 through 1984, and market shares for commercial lending do not appear to have changed dramatically since 1984. In contrast, commercial banks have taken a larger share of the mortgage market, principally at the expense of the savings and loan industry. The gain has been especially great in the commercial loan market.

Summary and Conclusions

Bank performance is important to individual consumers of bank deposit and loan services as well as to the performance of the entire economy. An effectively functioning financial system requires a banking system that can earn a reasonable return by taking an acceptable level of risk.

The banking system has experienced declining profitability and growing risk during the 1980s. The return on assets of banks of virtually any size group has fallen while the number of problem and failed banks has increased. These developments reflect the combined influence of a number of different factors, including inflation, high and volatile interest rates, changes in technology, more sophisticated consumers, deregulation, globalization of financial services, and the impact of new competitors. As a result, the competitive environment facing commercial banks at the beginning of the 1990s was fundamentally transformed from the one existing at the beginning of the 1980s. This makes an effective analysis of the financial conditions of commercial banks more difficult but also much more important.

2

The Dimensions of
Bank Performance

This chapter provides an overview of the two principal dimensions of bank performance: *profitability* and *risk*. Just as bank activities are multidimensional, so too are the measures of bank performance so it is necessary to discuss more than one aspect of profitability and risk. The focus here is on the two most commonly used measures of profitability: the Return on Assets (ROA) and the Return on Equity (ROE). Capturing the essence of the risk concept is more difficult because there are numerous dimensions of risk. Credit risk, interest rate risk, liquidity risk, capital risk, and fraud risk are explained here. In addition, the discussion covers other dimensions of bank performance such as technological risk, subsidiary risk, and operating-efficiency risk. It also provides information on the sources of data on bank performance.

An Overview

As with all business enterprises, commercial banks establish goals and make the decisions necessary to achieve most of those goals. The bank's principal goal is to maximize the value of the organization to its shareholders. For publicly traded banks, this amounts to making decisions which lead to an increase in the market value of the stock as traded in the financial markets. However, since most commercial banks do not have publicly traded stock, management must rely on other more obvious measures to indicate the bank is moving toward its goals–profitability and risk. Decisions which increase the profitability of the bank without increasing its risk will obviously make the bank more valuable to its shareholders. Similarly, decisions which reduce the risk of the bank without reducing its profitability will also increase the value of the shareholders' stake. Unfortunately, most decisions require a trade-off between profitability (or return) and risk. Increases in profitability are usually possible only through acceptance of greater risk, and reductions in risk can usually be achieved only through acceptance of lower profitability. Management's success in achieving its goals may be thought of in terms of the ability to balance profitability and risk in order to achieve the goals of the organization.

Balancing of risk and return occur through a number of financial and non-financial decisions and through both operational and portfolio management strategies. For example, a bank faces a choice as to replacing its existing computer system or its existing communications system. Perhaps a more expensive computer system would provide more rapid information and allow greater capacity to provide information usable to management in decision-making. Is the extra cost worth the extra capacity? Such a decision is not an easy one since many of the benefits are difficult to quantify. Yet the decision affects both the profitability and the risk of the organization and thereby the achievement of its ultimate goals.

Similarly, the bank faces a decision on alternative compensation systems. It could, for example, follow a strategy of paying above average salaries by employing a smaller workforce per dollar of assets. The expectation would be that the quality of service provided from this lean organization would more than compensate for the higher cost per employee. Another strategy would be to pay average or below average salaries, to emphasize quantity rather than quality. Each of these strategies obviously has important profitability and risk implications.

While the above two illustrations may seem only loosely related to the profitability and risk dimensions of bank performance, most portfolio management decisions are directly connected to these factors. For example, a bank could follow an investment strategy that used short term, large denomination certificates of deposit to fund a portfolio of long term fixed rate securities. Such a policy would work well in a period of falling interest rates–profitability would increase dramatically–and would do so at the expense of greater risk. Another bank may deliberately choose to make few loans to only the highest quality borrowers. Such a policy obviously reduces the risk of loan losses though it does so at the expense of lost profitability.

Figure 2-1 provides a framework for further understanding the necessary balance between profitability and risk that management must achieve. As indicated, the fundamental but often unobservable goal of maximizing shareholder wealth may be thought of in terms of its profitability and risk dimensions. Virtually all decisions made by bank management affect *both* profitability and risk, including decisions about computer operations, communications, personnel development, fixed asset acquisitions, portfolio management, lending policies, etc. Finding the appropriate balance of profitability and risk is the responsibility as well as the challenge of management.

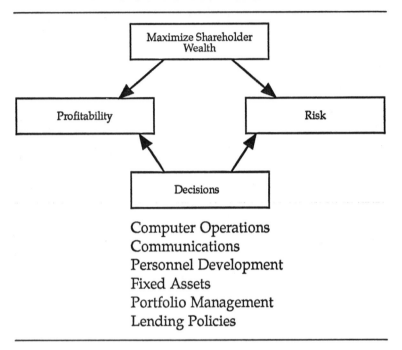

FIGURE 2-1
Profitability and Risk as
Dimensions of Bank Performance

Computer Operations
Communications
Personnel Development
Fixed Assets
Portfolio Management
Lending Policies

Bank management's success (or failure) in balancing profitability and risk may be analyzed by looking at the bank's financial statements. Much of this chapter is devoted to a discussion of how to achieve such a balance.

Profitability

The two most commonly used measures of bank profitability are the Return on Assets (ROA) and the Return on Equity (ROE). ROA may be calculated as shown in equation (1).

$$ROA = \frac{\text{Net Profit After Taxes}}{\text{Average Assets}} \qquad (1)$$

ROE may be calculated as shown in equation (2).

$$ROE = \frac{\text{Net Profit After Taxes}}{\text{Average Equity}} \qquad (2)$$

ROA measures management's effectiveness at utilizing its resources to generate profits. This measure of bank profitability is particularly relevant when comparing operating efficiencies across banks. As discussed in Chapter 1, ROAs for very large banks are usually less than ROA's for medium-sized banks.

While ROA does provide perspective on the ability of management to generate profit per dollar of assets invested, ROE may be a more relevant measure of performance for shareholders. ROE focuses on the ability of management to generate profits per dollar of shareholder's equity.

ROA and ROE may be related with the use of equation (3).

$$ROE = ROA \times \text{Leverage Multiplier} \qquad (3)$$

or

$$\frac{\text{Net Profit}}{\text{Average Equity}} = \frac{\text{Net Profit}}{\text{Average Assets}} \times \frac{\text{Average Assets}}{\text{Average Equity}} \qquad (4)$$

Equation (3) shows that the ROE is the product of ROA and the Leverage Multiplier (LM) where LM is the amount of average assets divided by the amount of average equity (the reciprocal of the ratio of equity to assets). While this is necessarily true in a mathematical sense as shown in equation (4), this simple relationship is quite important in understanding the profitability dimension of bank performance. For example, a bank with a low ROA may increase its ROE by using greater financial leverage by increasing the ratio of assets to equity (reducing the ratio of equity to assets). Large banks, for example, may increase their ROE to the level of smaller banks by increasing their assets per dollar of equity. Or, a bank may cushion the impact of a declining ROA on its ROE by increasing its leverage multiplier.

Table 2-1 illustrates further the relationship between ROA and ROE. For example, in year one, the bank has an ROA of .50 percent and a leverage multiplier of twenty. As a result, ROE is 10% (.50 x .20). In year two, ROA falls to .40 (perhaps because of an increase in the cost of funds due to deposit rate deregulation or from declining loan rates due to greater competition in the loan market). Bank management can offset the effect of the declining ROA on ROE by increasing the leverage multiplier from twenty to twenty-five. As a result, the ROE remains at ten percent. (Management has maintained a constant ROE, though at the expense of increasing the risk profile of the bank). In year three the ROA continues to shrink and once again the leverage multiplier is increased (to $33^{1}/3$) in order to maintain a constant ROE.

There is, though, a limit as to how high the leverage multiplier would be allowed to go. This limit most commonly would be established by the regulatory authorities—the Comptroller of the Currency, the FDIC, or the Federal Reserve System—who now specify minimum ratios of equity capital to assets (thereby establishing maximum ratios of assets to equity capital). Even in the absence of regulatory imposed limits on the use of financial leverage by bank management, however, limits may be imposed by financial markets or by management's own prudence.

TABLE 2-1

The Relationship Between ROA and ROE

ROE = ROA x LM

Year 1
    ROA = .50
    LM   = 20

    ROE = 10%

Year 2
    ROA = .40
    LM   = 25

    ROE = 10%

Year 3
    ROA = .30
    LM   = 33⅓

    ROE = 10%

Year 4
    ROA = .20
    LM   = 33⅓

    ROE =   6.66%

Year 5
    ROA = .20
    LM   = 25

    ROE =   5%

Assume that in year four, for whatever reason, the ROA continues to decline and falls to .20. If a leverage multiplier of 33^1/3 is the maximum possible, then the ROE will shrink to 6.66 percent. Further, assume in year five that the ROA stabilizes at .20 but that bank management is forced to (or chooses to) reduce the degree of financial leverage from 33^1/3 in year four to twenty-five in year five. Despite a constant ROA, the return on equity would fall to five percent.

Risk

Banks accept a number of different types of risk–credit, interest rate, liquidity, capital, and fraud–as they seek to obtain adequate returns on assets and equity. Each dimension of bank risk is discussed in turn, although the order in which they are described here does not necessarily imply an order of importance. In fact, the importance of each of these types of risk changes over time. In some periods, financial stress at banks primarily stems from credit risk while in other periods interest rate risk may be more significant.

Credit Risk refers to the possibility that the borrower will be unwilling or unable to meet the commitment to pay interest and repay principal. It encompasses both the prospect of nonpayment and delay of payment. With a positive time value of money, delay of payment results in a very real loss to the lender. Credit risk exists both for the loan portfolio of a commercial bank and for the securities portfolio, though credit losses are generally concentrated in the loan portfolio.

Table 2-2 provides information on the causes of bank failure as compiled by the FDIC. In addition, Table 2-2 provides this information classified by bank size, thereby providing insight as to whether the importance of the different risk factors vary for small as compared with large banks.

TABLE 2-2
Causes of Commercial Bank Failure by Size Decile, 1971-1982[1]

| | Size Decile | | | | | | | | | | | |
| | 1 (Small) | | 2 - 3 | | 4 - 5 | | 6 - 7 | | 8 - 9 | | 10 (Large) | |
Cause	Major	Primary	Major	Primary	Major	Primary	Major	Primary	Major	Primary	Major	Primary
Credit Quality Losses												
Loans	83%	66%	77%	65%	81%	62%	60%	47%	57%	43%	86%	66%
Insider Loans	31	10	26	10	38	19	67	27	43	29	33	10
Poor Funds Management												
Rate Sensitivity	14	0	10	3	24	9	13	0	14	0	48	14
Liquidity	35	0	36	3	24	0	33	0	29	0	57	10
Fraud and Embezzlement												
Internal	17	17	19	13	5	5	20	13	29	28	0	0
External	7	7	10	6	5	5	13	13	14	0	0	0
Proof		100		100		100		100		100		100
Number of cases (including assistance cases)		29		31		21		15		7		21

1. Causes are shown as a percentage of the number of failures for each size group. Major refers to all causes noted in each failure. Since most banks fail for more than one reason, the total of the "Major" column exceeds 100 percent. "Primary" refers to the one case in each case that seemed most important.

Source: Federal Deposit Insurance Corporation, *Deposit Insurance in a Changing Environment*, (Washington, D.C.: FDIC, 1983): 11-17.

The cause of bank failure listed as "loans" perhaps relates most closely to the concept of credit risk. The primary cause of failure refers to the one cause in each failure that appeared to be most important. The major cause of failure refers to all the various causes of failure and may therefore exceed 100 percent for any failure.

As shown in Table 2-2, the primary cause of bank failures was credit risk–with loan losses accounting for failure in most of the 124 banks studied by the FDIC. There doesn't appear to be a particular trend in the principal causes of bank failure as shown in Table 2-2; loan losses seem to dominate for any of the subperiods shown in that table.

The extent of the difficulties that a commercial bank is experiencing with the credit risk dimension of its portfolio can be found by looking at the volume of its charge-offs. When a loan is deemed by management to be uncollectible (or when the regulatory authorities make such a decision), that loan is expunged or "charged off" from the bank balance sheet. This does not mean, of course, that the bank stops trying to collect on the loan. In fact, active programs are normally maintained to collect charged-off loans and a large percentage of previously charged-off loans is frequently collected. Hence, the analyst is interested not only in the amount of gross charge-offs but also in the amount of net charge-offs (gross charge-off less recoveries).

A particularly important device used to gauge the degree of credit risk at a commercial bank is the volume of nonperforming assets–those that exhibit unusually high degrees of credit risk and therefore may be used as useful predictors of future charge-offs. Increases in nonperforming loans are usually followed by increases in loan charge-offs. Nonperforming assets are the sum of (1) nonaccrual loans; (2) restructured loans; 3) past due loans, and (4) other loan related assets. The first three of these four categories are nonperforming loans. Nonaccrual loans are those loans where payment of principal and/or interest is doubtful and as a result accrual of interest has been suspended. Restructured loans are those loans in which the terms have been renegotiated (generally with a lower interest rate and/or a longer maturity). Past due loans are those which are contractually past due 90 days or more as to interest or principal payments. Other loan related assets, usually real estate, are assets that have been obtained from distressed borrowers in partial satisfaction of a loan agreement.

Interest Rate Risk–the effect of changes in interest rate levels on the profitability of the bank–is another of the important risks that bank management faces in structuring their bank's portfolio. Increases in interest rates may lead to higher profits, lower profits, or no change in bank profits. The effects of interest rate changes on bank profits depend on the structure of the assets and liabilities chosen by bank management. In particular, the effects of fluctuating interest rates depend on the relative magnitude of interest rate sensitive assets and interest rate sensitive liabilities.

Important rate sensitive assets (RSA) are those whose interest rate will change with changes in the general level of interest rates within a specified time horizon (often called the planning horizon). These rate sensitive assets would include any variable rate asset as well as those assets that mature within the specified time period. Together, RSAs may also be referred to as repriceable-assets. Interest rate sensitive liabilities (RSL) are those whose interest costs will change with changes in the general level of interest rates within a specified time period (the planning horizon). These include both variable rate liabilities (of which there are very few) as well as those liabilities that mature within the specified time period.

The interest rate sensitivity position of a bank depends upon the relative magnitude of rate sensitive assets and rate sensitive liabilities. The difference between the two is referred to as the gap and may be calculated as shown in equation (5).

$$\$Gap = \$RSA - \$RSL \qquad (5)$$

where the dollar gap is the difference between the volume of rate sensitive assets and rate sensitive liabilities. The gap may also be expressed in relative terms, as shown in equation (6).

$$Relative\ Gap = \frac{\$Gap}{Earning\ Assets} \qquad (6)$$

whereby the dollar gap amount is divided by the volume of earning assets. This ratio standardizes the amount of the gap thereby providing a more meaningful comparison of the gap from one bank to another or for one bank over time. The relationship between interest sensitive assets and liabilities may also be expressed in ratio form (equation (7)) as the interest sensitivity ratio (ISR), where

$$Interest\ Sensitivity\ Ratios = \frac{\$RSA}{\$RSL} \qquad (7)$$

or the interest sensitivity ratio is equal to the dollar amount of interest sensitive assets divided by the dollar amount of interest sensitive liabilities.

The relationship between the interest sensitivity position of a bank's portfolio and the effect of changing interest rates on a bank's portfolio are shown in Table 2-3. Banks with a positive gap (interest sensitive assets that exceed interest sensitive liabilities–an interest sensitive ratio of more than one) will find that their profits increase or decrease directly with changes in interest rates. Increasing interest rates will produce rising profits for these *asset sensitive* institutions while falling interest rates will produce declining profits. In contrast, banks with a negative gap (interest sensitive assets that are less than interest sensitive liabilities–an interest sensitivity ratio of less than one) will find that their profits decrease or increase inversely with changes in interest rates. Increases in interest rates will produce falling profits for these *liability sensitive* institutions while falling interest rates will produce increasing profits.

Bank management may offset the effect of changing interest rates by managing the interest sensitivity position of the bank's portfolio in order to achieve a small gap position. As shown in Table 2-3, the bank with a zero gap (rate sensitive assets equal to rate sensitive liabilities–an interest sensitivity

---

TABLE 2-3
Interest Rates, Bank Profits, and
The Interest Sensitivity Position

	Interest Sensitivity Position	Interest Rates	Bank Profitability
Dollar Gap	Interest Sensitivity Ratio		
Positive ($RSA–$RSL>0)	More than one $\dfrac{\$RSA}{\$RSL} > 1$	Rising Falling	Rising Falling
Negative ($RSA–$RSL<0)	Less than one $\dfrac{\$RSA}{\$RSL} < 1$	Rising Falling	Falling Rising
Zero ($RSA–$RSL = 0)	One $\dfrac{\$RSA}{\$RSL} = 1$	Rising Falling	No Change No Change

---

ratio of one) could (theoretically though not practically) isolate the profitability position of the bank from changes in interest rates. Increases or decreases in interest rates should have little effect on profitability for a bank with a zero gap (and an interest sensitivity ratio of one).

As shown in Table 2-2, interest rate risk has played a very minor role in bank failures, at least through 1982. For the entire 1971-1982 period, interest rate risk was the primary cause of failure in less than five percent of the cases. The importance of interest rate risk as a cause of failure, though, appears to have increased somewhat in more recent years, rising to 5.8 percent as the primary cause of failure in 1980-82 and 8.8 percent in 1982, possibly reflecting the greater volatility of interest rates in the early 1980s. It is also interesting (and somewhat surprising) to note in Table 2-1 that interest rate risk was a primary cause of bank failures only for those banks in the largest decile of the bank failure group. Large banks, with more sophisticated personnel and greater ability to adjust their portfolios with a variety of asset and liability vehicles, might have been expected to be less affected by interest rate movements. These data suggest, however, that larger banks are willing to take greater interest rate risk in their pursuit of profitability.

The interest rate risk of commercial banks differs considerably from that of savings and loans and savings banks. Commercial banks have been able to match the maturity or interest rate sensitivity of their assets and liabilities quite well. Savings and loans and savings banks, however, have found it much more difficult to manage interest rate risk, perhaps reflecting their historical role of borrowing short term and lending long term. These differences are shown in Tables 2-4 and 2-5. Commercial banks, for example, as shown in Table 2-4, had a one year gap of -7.8 percent of total assets

TABLE 2-4
Repricing Information for FDIC - Insured Commercial Banks and FSLIC - Insured Savings and Loans and Savings Banks. Year-End 1987 ($Billions).

COMMERCIAL BANKS

	Maturity or Earliest Time to Repricing		
	1 year or less	1 year- 5 years	over 5 years
Selected Assets[1]	$1613	$ 619	$342
Selected Liabilities[2]	1846	166	20
Incremental Gap	-233	453	
Cumulative Gap	233	220	
As percent of Total Assets:	one-year	five-year	
Cumulative Gap	-7.8	7.3	

SAVINGS AND LOANS AND SAVINGS BANKS

	Maturity or Earliest Time to Repricing		
	1 year or less	1 year- 5 years	over 5 years
Selected Assets[1]	$ 477	$ 146	$498
Selected Liabilities	840	212	43
Incremental Gap	-363	-65	
Cumulative Gap	-363	-428	
As percent of Total Assets:	one-year	five-year	
Cumulative Gap	-29.0	-34.2	

1. Excludes assets held in trading accounts, equity securities, nonaccruing assets, intangible assets, fixed assets and miscellaneous other assets.

2. Excludes $456 billion in demand deposits and $177 billion in "passbook" savings deposits as well as $154 billion of miscellaneous liabilities. Includes NOWs and MMDAs in "less than one year" repricing interval.

Source: George E. French, "Measuring the Interest Rate Exposure of Financial Intermediaries," *FDIC Banking Review*, Vol., No. 1, (Fall 1988): 22.

TABLE 2-5
Quartile Distribution of Gap Estimates of Interest Rate Exposure for FDIC Insured Commercial Banks and FSLIC Insured Savings and Loans and Savings Banks, Year End 1987.

FDIC-INSURED COMMERCIAL BANKS			
	Lower	Median	Upper
As percent of assets:			
1-year gap	-18.3	-8.7	0.8
5-year gap	4.2	12.2	19.6

FSLIC-INSURED S&LS AND SAVINGS BANKS			
	Lower	Median	Upper
As percent of assets:			
1-year gap	-41.0	-28.7	-16.8
5-year gap	-45.5	-30.3	-16.7

Source: George E. French, "Measuring the Interest Rate Exposure of Financial Intermediaries," *FDIC Banking Review*, Vol. No. 1 (Fall 1988): 23.

---

while the five year gap was +7.3 percent. In contrast, savings and loans and savings banks had a -29.0 percent one year gap and an even larger -34.2 percent five year gap.

The differences between interest rate exposure for commercial banks and thrifts is shown even more dramatically in Table 2-5. For the twenty-five percent of banks with the greatest one year gap, the average gap was -18.3 percent of assets. In contrast, for the twenty-five percent of thrifts with the greatest one year gap, the average gap was -41.0 percent.

Liquidity Risk refers to the need for adequate liquidity in order to meet withdrawal demands by depositors and other creditors and to provide funds to meet the legitimate demands of borrowers. Failure to provide adequate liquidity to meet the demands of depositors and nondeposits or creditors obviously results in a liquidity crisis and can shut a bank down within a very short period. The effects of failure to provide adequate liquidity for potential loan customers presents the bank with a longer term but no less serious problem than that of inadequate deposit liquidity.

Banks may obtain liquidity to meet the demands of depositors or borrowers either from liquidating assets (asset liquidity) or from borrowing (liability liquidity). Asset liquidity may be proxied by measuring the volume of short term and highly liquid assets held by a bank. Conceptually, this would include short term securities not required to be pledged to secure government deposits as well as anticipated collections on loans. In terms of ratios, asset liquidity may be (equation (8) measured as:

$$\text{Asset Liquidity} = \frac{\text{Short Term nonpledged Securities + Anticipated Collections from loans}}{\text{Total Deposits}} \qquad (8)$$

Liability liquidity is much more difficult to measure than asset liquidity. Conceptually, it is the difference between the maximum amount that a bank could borrow (through use of the federal funds market, the market for large–jumbo–CD's or other means) and the amount of borrowings that it currently has outstanding. In terms of ratios, liability liquidity may be calculated as shown in equation (9):

$$\text{Liability Liquidity} = \frac{\text{Maximum Borrowing Capacity} - \text{Current (actual) Borrowings}}{\text{Total Deposits}} \qquad (9)$$

Liability liquidity would therefore be reduced by an increase in the current level of borrowing or by a reduction in the borrowing capacity of the bank. The latter part of the liability liquidity calculation is difficult to estimate. Moreover, and of more significance, when a bank experiences financial difficulties (due to credit risk problems, for example) the maximum borrowing capacity of the bank usually declines dramatically. At the extreme, the borrowing capacity of a bank may evaporate, resulting in that bank having to rely entirely upon the volume of its assets for liquidity. Since large banks rely principally on liability liquidity in order to meet their deposit and loan requirements, financial difficulties caused by credit quality problems can quickly cause a financial crisis.

Liquidity problems are not generally a primary cause of bank failure (See Table 2-2). They were, in fact, the primary cause of bank failure in less than three percent of the cases in the 1970-1982 period. Liquidity problems did, however tend to be a more significant reason for larger bank failure, most likely reflecting their more aggressive use of liability management. While not the primary source, liquidity was a major cause of bank failures. For example, in the 1971-1982 period, liquidity risk was a major cause of bank failure in over twenty-six percent of the cases. For the largest ten percent of the failed banks, liquidity risk was a major cause of failure in fifty-seven percent of the cases.

Capital (or leverage) Risk refers to the extent to which a bank's assets may fall in value before the position of depositors and other creditors is threatened. For example, a bank with a five percent ratio of equity capital to total assets could not experience a fall in the value of its assets by more than five percent without becoming insolvent (having the value of its assets reduced to less than the value of its liabilities). In contrast, a bank with a ten percent ratio of equity to assets could experience a five percent shrinkage in the value of its assets without becoming insolvent. The amount of capital risk is usually measured by the equity capital ratio as shown in equation (10):

$$\text{Capital Risk} \atop \text{(equity capital ratio)} \quad = \quad \frac{\text{Equity Capital}}{\text{Assets}} \qquad (10)$$

where equity capital is the amount of common and preferred stock, surplus, retained earnings, and reserve for loan losses (and other purposes).

The higher the ratio of equity capital to assets, the lower the degree of risk. Of course, the ratio of equity capital to assets is the reciprocal of the leverage multiplier that was discussed earlier. As a bank increases its equity capital ratio (thereby reducing its risk) it decreases its leverage multiplier and lowers the return on equity for any given return on assets.

FDIC data cited in Table 2-2 do not explicitly point to capital risk as a cause of bank failure. Instead, they focus on the causes of the shrinkage in bank asset value, such as credit quality problems, that would place strain on the capital position and thereby on the solvency of a bank. Most studies suggest, however, that capital is not a sufficient defense against these other types of risk and that even large amounts of capital are usually inadequate to prevent the failure of a bank with severe risk problems. The exhaustion of capital, then, is the ultimate result of losses produced by excessive credit, interest rate, and liquidity risk.

Fraud Risk. Bank failures also result from theft by internal management and external fraud such as a bank paying on uncollected funds (check-kiting schemes being the most common example). Closely related to these dimensions of risk is the risk of insider loans in which the bank has an excessive volume of loans outstanding to officers and directors. Losses on these loans may or may not be associated with fraudulent activities.

Fraud and embezzlement, as shown in Table 2-2, have been a significant cause of bank failures. In fact, internal and external fraud and embezzlement were the primary causes in almost 17 percent of bank failures in the 1971-1982 period. Insider loans were the primary cause of 44.5 percent of the failures over the same period. Of particular importance–there appears to be a strong relationship between bank size and the importance of fraud and embezzlement as a cause of failure. For example, as shown in Table 2-2, not one of the largest ten percent of the failed banks was declared insolvent due to internal or external fraud and embezzlement. In contrast, for the smallest ten percent of the failed banks, fraud and embezzlement constituted the primary cause of failure in almost one-quarter of the cases. The importance of insider loans as a source of failure, however, was not related to bank size in this way. These data do suggest that the prediction of bank failures using financial statement data should be more accurate for large banks than for small.

Detection of fraud risk is difficult, both for those inside a banking organization and for the outside observer when using only the bank's financial statements. One useful index of fraud risk, however, is the extent of loans to insiders, including officers, directors, and major shareholders. One recent study which examined the failure rate of banks that had lent an amount equal to more than twenty-five percent of their assets to insiders discovered their failure rate to be nearly four times higher than that of other banks. In fact, the five banks that had the highest rates of insider loans in 1986 have since failed.[1]

The FDIC recently reported on the importance of fraud in a sample of 218 bank failures. In roughly twenty-five percent of the failures, the bank examiners detected the presence of fraud or insider abuse.[2] This doesn't necessarily imply that the fraud or insider abuse were the principal or even subsidiary causes of failure, only that fraud appeared to exist in these fifty-four banks. The average size of the failed banks in which fraud or insider abuse were present was $29.5 million, not greatly different from the average size ($32 million) for the failed banks without fraud or insider abuse. Additionally, the average loss on assets for failed banks in which fraud was present was not greater than the average asset loss for failed banks in which fraud was not present–31.6 percent versus 34.2 percent. Similarly, the loss to the FDIC did not differ between the two–27.9 percent for the failed banks in which fraud was present and 30.7 percent for the failed banks in which fraud was not present.

Other Dimensions of Risk

While our discussion of credit, interest rate, liquidity, capital, and fraud risk provides a reasonably comprehensive description of the major types of bank risk, there are a number of other risk dimensions that should also be considered–*management risk, delivery risk*, and *off balance sheet risk.*

Management risk refers to the (presumably) few but extraordinary failures that may arise from management error

---

1. Edward Lawrence, Donald Kummer, and Nasser Arshadi,"Inside Borrowing Practices of Commercial Banks," *Issues in Bank Regulation*, (Summer 1987): 28–33

2 . See John Bovenzi and Arthur Morton, "Resolution Cost of Bank Failures," *FDIC Banking Review*, Vol. 1, No. 1 (Fall 1988): 9.

in the use of the new powers that have been given to banks and other financial institutions in a deregulated environment. With the essential completion of deposit rate deregulation in 1986, and the gradual move toward additional product and geographical diversification, bank management has the power to make very good and very bad decisions. The very bad decisions may involve incorrect pricing of deposits, the offering of new and unprofitable products, the opening of branches in undesirable locations, or the purchasing of banks at excessive premiums. These errors ultimately will show up in the financial statement of the bank and will produce reduced profits and increased risk. Impact on financial statements may, however, be delayed for a considerable period of time, perhaps years.

Closely related to management risk is strategic risk–the risk of failure stemming from an incorrect strategic management policy adopted by the senior management and/or board of directors of a banking organization. Continental Illinois provides a good example of strategic risk. This bank embarked on a rapid growth strategy in the late 1970's. The strategy appeared to be successful until 1982, when the failure of Penn Square Bank and the revelation that Continental Illinois had purchased large amounts of low quality loans from Penn Square called that strategy into question. While the identification of strategic risk is quite difficult, the long-run implication of fundamentally incorrect strategies may be catastrophic for bank financial performance.

Banks also face *delivery risk* when performing their role as financial intermediaries.[3] This risk concept, which looks at banks not as portfolios of assets and liabilities, but as deliv-

---

3 . This concept of risk is developed by Sinkey. See Joseph J. Sinkey, Jr., "Risk Regulation in the Banking Industry," *Federal Reserve Bank of Chicago Proceedings of the 1984 Conference on Bank Structure and Competition*, (May 1984): 452-460.

ery vehicles for financial services, is composed of three parts: *technological risk, subsidiary risk,* and *operating-efficiency risk.* *Technological risk* refers to the inherent risk involved in the introduction of electronic and telecommunications equipment into banking. Given the large amount of dollars banks have invested in new equipment and the rapid changes in technology, it appears likely that technological risk has increased, perhaps substantially. Subsidiary risk refers to the risk encountered by banks as they increase their product lines through geographic expansion, product expansion, joint ventures and other devices. Such expansions are frequently implemented through a subsidiary of a bank holding company and will increase as bank holding companies diversify through their subsidiaries into new ventures. Operating efficiency risk is related to economies of scale and scope and refers to the risk that stems from a bank's inability to provide financial services at competitive costs. While, as with management risk, delivery risk is difficult to identify (though it is ultimately reflected in financial statements), it is important to analyze these dimensions of banking risk in order to properly evaluate bank financial performance.

Off-Balance Sheet Banking (OBSB) and the risk that it produces have literally exploded in recent years as commercial banking organizations have sought ways to earn income (usually fee income) without producing assets or liabilities on the bank's balance sheet. In a general sense, OBSB refers to the use of contingent claims or contracts whereby the bank agrees to make a loan under certain circumstances. These contingent claims generate fee income but do not affect the bank's balance sheet until and unless the contingency is realized and the loan actually made.

The most common OBSB activities are loan commitments and standby letters of credit, though operations of commercial banks in interest rate and foreign currency swaps and futures trading are also significant. Loan commitments exceeded $500 billion at U.S. banks in 1986 while standby letters of credit approximated $200 billion.

Loan commitments are legally binding agreements to lend a borrower a specified amount for a specified purpose, generally at a stipulated rate. In effect, the bank is providing an insurance policy guaranteeing that the potential borrower will have access to funds. The Note Issuance Facility (NIF) is one of the most common types of loan commitments. With a NIF, the bank agrees to purchase the short-term commercial paper of a borrower or to provide funds if the borrower cannot sell notes at an interest rate at which the bank would provide credit. For this option, the potential borrower pays a fee to the bank.

A standby letter of credit is similar to a loan commitment except that it involves a third party. With a standby letter of credit, the bank commits to a third party that if its customer cannot provide funds to meet the terms and conditions of a financial contract, it (the bank) will make the commitment good. Standby letters of credit are used as backup lines of credit to support commercial paper offerings, municipal borrowings, construction lending, and mergers and acquisitions. Banks receive a fee for the standby letter as well as interest if the loan is actually made.

A number of factors account for the sharp increase in off balance sheet banking. Regulatory factors (in particular the lack of capital required behind off balance sheet assets and liabilities) have undoubtedly played a role. Reserve requirements and deposit insurance factors also encourage OBSB (recent regulatory changes will, when fully implemented, require capital for OBSB assets and liabilities). The declining profitability at major banks and growing competition from other lenders also seem important. Certainly the ability to generate fee income by issuing financial guarantees is attractive to many banks. Yet the existence of hundreds of billions of dollars of liabilities for the banking system that do not show up on their balance sheets raises important questions about the future stability of this nation's banks.

High Performance Banks

Commercial banks differ widely in their portfolio management strategies as well as the economic environments within which they operate. Reflecting these differences, the profitability and risk dimensions of banks also vary greatly. Yet there is evidence indicating that some banks have been able to achieve consistently high performance. What are the characteristics of these banks and their strategies? Although not a great deal is known about these high performance banks, there is some evidence concerning their characteristics.

One study of high performance banks focused on the top 3000 performing FDIC insured banks over the 1978-1982 period, using ROA as the index of profitability.[4] All identified banks had consistently performed above the median for banks in their state over the five year period of the study. Included in the study were not only analyses of the financial ratios of these banks, but also discussions with the senior managers about strategic positions and management philosophies.

Banks in the study serve different geographic areas with different economic environments, yet they were able to obtain ROAs consistently above the norm for the industry.

4. Robert Holt and Karen Walewski, "Consistent High Performance Banks, 1978-1982, " *The Magazine of Bank Administration*, (April 1984): 75-78.

Why? There appear to be a number of underlying factors. First, these high performance banks were able to earn an average ROA of 1.67 percent (compared to 1.11 percent for the banking industry as a whole) and an average ROE of 16.74 percent (versus 12.94 percent for all banks) because they: (1) effectively managed the asset-liability of their portfolio and the risks involved in the balance sheet and (2) aggressively priced their noninterest fee-based services based upon perceived high quality service. Other characteristics of the high performance banks included greater use of large denomination liabilities, and greater amounts of earning assets (as a fraction of total assets).

A second study was done at the Federal Reserve Bank of Dallas assessing average annual return on assets (ROA) over the 1981-1985 period.[5] Since many bank financial ratios vary with the size of the organization, banks in the sample were divided into three groups: (1) small banks with total assets from $25-$100 million, (2) mid-size banks with total assets from $100-$250 million, and (3) large banks with more than $250 million in total assets. Four types of strategies were examined:

1. Investment strategy: percentage of total assets allocated to eight categories of loans and two categories of assets. The related ratios of loan interest income and total income were calculated also.

2. Funding strategy: percentage of total assets funded by transactions deposits, savings and small time deposits, large time deposits, foreign deposits, and borrowed funds.

3. Growth strategy: overall growth of total assets.

---

5. Robert Clair, "Financial Strategies of Top-Performance Banks in the Eleventh District," *Federal Reserve Bank of Dallas Economic Review*, (January 1987): 1-13.

4. Off-balance sheet strategy: percentage of total assets allocated to loan and lease commitments and letters of credit and to commitments on forward, future, and option contracts. These measures were intended to capture management's usage of noninterest, service income, which was also directly measured as the ratio of noninterest income to total income.

The following results of comparisons between top and low performing banks were obtained:

1. Two successful financial strategies were the commercial real estate strategy and the conservative strategy. The former involved relatively higher lending in commercial real estate, lower lending in commercial and industrial loans, and higher lending to consumers. The conservative strategy was associated with low credit risks and strong asset liquidity.

   A third group of top performers did not use any distinct financial strategy but did tend to control their expenses better than other banks.

2. Regardless of financial strategy, top performers had lower loan losses than low performers.

3. Among small banks, top performers acquired a larger or smaller proportion of funds from transactions accounts (small savings and time deposit accounts) than low performers.

4. Among large banks, top performers tended to use a lower proportion of borrowed funds than low performers.

5. Financial strategies are affected by cyclical changes in business conditions (e.g., the success of the commercial real estate strategy is related to the growth of the commercial construction business). As such, banks

should adapt their strategies based on economic forecasts.

The data used in the Clair study of the financial ratios of high performing banks in the 11th (Dallas) Federal Reserve District were drawn from 1981-85 bank financial statements which reflect economic conditions prior to the 1986 collapse of oil prices. Whether the patterns of financial ratios observed for high performance banks continued in 1986 and beyond is an important question, but unfortunately one that has no answer. It is, however, interesting to note that the top performing banks in the Clair study pursued very rapid growth strategies. For example, the average small bank increased its total assets by 96.3 percent over the period from 1981 to 1985. Yet, as will be discussed more extensively in chapter 6, there is evidence that banks that are growing more rapidly than their peers are more likely to experience financial distress.

A third study was done by Watro at the Federal Reserve Bank of Cleveland.[6] In this study, all banks in Ohio, Pennsylvania, Kentucky, and West Virginia that achieved an ROA of more than two percent in 1983 were compared with those banks that failed to earn a positive profit in the same year.[6] Comparisons were made between high profit and low profit banks in terms of their financial ratios such as revenue on loans and securities, costs of funds, and noninterest revenue and expense, as well as the size and ownership characteristics of the bank. The comparisons yielded the following conclusions:

1. The high profit banks generally made fewer loans than the low profit banks. In fact, high earnings banks held only 39.2 percent of their assets in loans while the low

---

6. Paul Watro, "Bank Earnings: Comparing the Extremes," *Federal Reserve Bank of Cleveland Economic Commentary*, (November 15, 1985): 1-4.

profit banks held 50.1 percent of their assets in loans. High profit banks made less business loans, but more real estate loans.

2. High profit banks were able to obtain funds at lower costs than the low profit banks. In fact, high profit banks' cost of funds averaged one percentage point less than low profit banks. Noninterest expenses were also substantially less.

3. High profit banks were less likely to be affiliated with a holding company than low profit banks.

4. Bank size was unimportant. Small banks were apparently quite able to compete with large banks.

Watro updated his study in order to determine whether the characteristics of high profit banks had been affected by deregulation and other financial trends in the 1980s.[7] He selected as his sample those banks in Ohio that, based on Return on Assets, ranked in the top twenty percent of all Ohio banks over either the 1973-77 or the 1983-87 period compared with the low earning banks which ranked in the bottom twenty percent. He found that:

1. high earning banks were quite successful in capitalizing on the opportunities that arise from a less regulated banking environment. These banks apparently were able to earn high returns without any significant rise in earnings volatility.

2. cost containment continues to be the key for achieving consistently high earnings.

3. high-earning banks held a larger share of their assets in securities and a smaller share in both loans, promises and other fixed assets, both before and after deregulation.

---

7. Paul Watro, "Have the Characteristics of High-Earning Banks Changed? Evidence from Ohio," *Federal Reserve Bank of Cleveland Economic Commentary,* (September 1, 1989):1-4.

Taking a longer term perspective, Wall examined independent (i.e., not affiliated with a holding company) banks that had consistent profitability records over a ten year period ending in 1982 and had total assets between $50 and $500 million.[8] His results, in general, are consistent with those of the previous studies. He concluded:

> The most profitable banks hold more securities, which reduces their non-interest expenses while earning the same revenue as more costly sources. They rely more on equity funding, which reduces their interest and non-interest expenses. They have more demand deposits, which reduce their interest expense. Finally, the difference between the most profitable and the less profitable banks' non-interest costs is so large that variations in the banks' asset and liability portfolio cannot explain the difference. This suggests that the most profitable banks maintain better cost controls. (p. 47)

Market Evaluation of Bank Performance

Analyzing the income statement and balance sheet of an individual commercial bank is an important part of assessing the performance of the institution. However, from the perspective of shareholders, depositors and other creditors, and of other analysts, useful information on the performance of the institution can be provided by looking at the market price of its securities. Changes over time in the prices of one bank's securities relative to those of other banks provide important information on the market's view of the profitabil-

8. Larry D. Wall, "Why Are Some Banks More Profitable?" *Federal Reserve Bank of Atlanta Economic Review*, (September 1983): 42-48.

ity and risk dimensions of a bank's performance. Unfortunately, market prices are available for only a small percentage of commercial banks. For those banks that have publicly traded securities, however, the bank analyst has an extremely valuable source of information.

Information on the market assessment of bank performance is available both from the equity and debt securities of a commercial bank. Increases in the price of a bank's stock should reflect either increases in the expected profitability of the organization or decreases in expected risk. The data provided on profitability and risk from the bank's financial statements are historical and reflect past management decisions; the data from the equity market are forward looking and reflect what the market expects to happen to the bank.

Bank performance information can also be found by looking at the bank's cost of deposits and nondeposit liabilities. If the cost of funds to the bank through issuance of deposits or selling of bonds increases (relative to the overall cost of funds in the financial markets), this is a signal that the market feels that the risk of the organization has increased.

Sources of Information on Bank Performance

Most information relating to bank financial performance comes from financial data provided by the banks themselves either directly or indirectly through the bank regulatory authorities or the Securities and Exchange Commission (SEC). All commercial banks insured by the FDIC (which include almost all banks) must file Reports of Condition (balance sheets) and Reports of Income with their primary supervision (Comptroller of the Currency, FDIC or Federal Reserve). The reports are filed on a quarterly basis. While the general format of the reports is similar, some differences exist based on a bank's size and the nature of its business. The federal banking agencies have made these reports public since the early 1970's.

The Uniform Bank Performance Report is one of the most useful sources of information on bank financial performance. This report, available to the public since December 1981, provides financial ratios derived from the most recent and four preceding call reports for individual banks. The report not only provides ratios for the individual bank, but also the median value for the most recent call date for a reference group of the bank's peers, together with the percentile level at which the bank's ratio falls within the peer group. This allows the analyst to place the performance of the bank under study in perspective to that of other comparable banks.

The Financial Institutions Regulatory and Interest Rate Control Act (FIRA) of 1978 requires that all insured banks report to their regulatory authorities annually on the amount of their loans to insiders. Information on the indebtedness of principal shareholders and executive officers who were indebted to the bank or its correspondent banks in the past calendar year must be reported. Both the reporting bank and its bank regulator are required to make the report public on request.

Those banks with publicly held securities face another set of disclosure regulations. As a result of the 1964 amendments to the Securities Exchange Act of 1934, appropriate securities laws are applicable to banks with more than $1 million in assets and a class of equity securities held by more than 500 stockholders or with a class of securities listed on an exchange. Enforcement of these regulations was assigned to the bank regulatory agencies. However, less than five percent (about 200) of insured commercial banks are "registered" under the 1934 act.

Most large (and many small) banking organizations are registered as bank holding companies which are subject to reporting requirements similar to those of commercial banks. Those institutions organized as bank holding companies must submit financial reports to the Federal Reserve System as required by the Bank Holding Company Act of 1956. These reports are generally available to the public. The Annual Report of Domestic Bank Holding Companies (y-6) contains consolidated bank holding company financial reports and parent-only financial statements as well as financial statements for each nonbank subsidiary. However, the y-6 report does not provide information on the bank subsidiaries of the holding company. In addition, holding companies with total consolidated assets of $50 million or more must file the Bank Holding Company Financial Supplement (y-9) which provides balance sheet and income statement information.

The SEC also administers the reporting and disclosure requirements under securities laws for bank holding companies. Holding companies must register any public sale (except for very small sales) of debt or equity with the SEC and provide a prospectus. Publicly held holding companies must be registered with the SEC in the same way that applies to publicly held banks. Publicly held holding companies must provide their shareholders with proxy statements and annual reports (including financial statements) and must file quarterly financial information with the SEC. This information is available to the public.

Federal securities laws also require disclosure of any outstanding cease-and-desist orders along with a description of the underlying condition within the bank which gave rise to the order. In the late 1970s, the FDIC began to publish summaries of its enforcement activities. Effective January 1,

1980, the Federal Financial Institutions Examination Council extended this policy to activities taken by all the federal regulatory authorities, although the name of the bank is deleted from such summaries. However, individual bank disclosure of this information can be obtained through the Freedom of Information Act.

There are a number of additional sources of information about the financial condition and performance of commercial banks. Rand McNally's *International Bank Directory*, for example, provides balance sheet information twice a year on U.S. and foreign banks as well as descriptive information on the location of the bank and its branches, and information on the officers and directors.

Several publishers issue financial ratios drawn from the Reports of Condition and Income filed by insured commercial banks. The Uniform Bank Performance Report used in this book is one of the most readily available. In addition, Sheshunoff and Company of Austin, Texas publishes extensive financial ratios and comparisons of financial ratios for individual banks. The analysis is provided for banks in each of the fifty states. Federal regulatory authorities (the Office of the Comptroller of the Currency, the FDIC, and the Federal Reserve System) also publish financial ratio data for groups of banks, such as those in various states, within different size groups.

Summary and Conclusions

Profitability and *risk* are the two dimensions affecting the performance of banking organizations. Banks attempt to earn an acceptable return on their assets or equity capital without taking excessive amounts of risk. This is a balancing act since, in most circumstances, increases in profitability are possible only by taking greater risk.

The two most common measures of bank profitability are the Return on Assets (ROA) and the Return on Equity (ROE), related through the Leverage Multiplier. While the principal dimensions of profitability are relatively easy to measure, risk is a much more difficult concept to proxy. Partially, this is due to the multiple dimensions of risk. Risk for banking organizations encompasses credit risk, interest rate risk, liquidity risk, capital risk, and fraud risk. Even more difficult to measure are the management, delivery, and off-balance sheet dimensions of risk. No matter how difficult to measure, however, the analyst must examine each of these dimensions of risk to properly evaluate the financial position of a banking organization.

3

Presentation of Bank Financial Statements

The Balance Sheet and the Income Statement

Understanding bank financial statements is an essential ingredient in the process of evaluating bank performance. Financial statements for banking institutions, unlike comparable information for most other types of business firms, are available in a uniform and consistent format that greatly facilitates comprehension. Although financial statements of nonbank business firms are prepared in accordance with generally accepted accounting principles, they can vary considerably in content and presentation. Making comparisons among companies or tracking a single firm over several years can be difficult as a result of the lack of uniformity. And, if a firm is not publicly traded, financial statements may not even be available for external analysis.

Balance sheets and income statements for all insured banks in the U.S. are compiled and published in a standardized document, the Uniform Bank Performance Report.[1] The

---

1 . The format of the Uniform Bank Performance Report changes over time; the description of the Uniform Bank Performance Report used in this book is the report format of January 1990. Report formats may also vary slightly depending upon the type of bank.

sources for all bank financial data in the Uniform Bank Performance Report are the Report of Condition and Report of Income filed quarterly with the appropriate regulatory agency:

- national banks, regulated by the Comptroller of the Currency;
- state banks, members of the Federal Reserve System, regulated by the Federal Reserve Board; and
- state-chartered banks, not members of the Federal Reserve System, regulated by the FDIC.

The Uniform Bank Performance Report presents financial statement information for individual banks on a quarterly and annual basis. Figure 3-1 shows a sample first page from the Uniform Bank Performance Report. In addition to the balance sheet and income statement data for the bank, the document presents key financial ratios and percentile rankings based on financial statements, and provides comparative financial statements and ratios for the bank's peer group. Peer group data are included to show the condition and performance of a group of banks with similar characteristics. The Uniform Bank Performance Report thus provides information that facilitates evaluation of an institution's current condition, how this condition has changed over time, an historical record of the bank's performance in major categories, and a comparison of the bank's financial record with other banks of comparable size and economic environment.

Provided free of charge on a quarterly basis to all federally insured commercial banks in the United States, each Uniform Bank Performance Report contains approximately twenty pages of bank financial data and peer group averages. The same report can be purchased by the general public from the Federal Financial Institutions Examination Council, UBPR, Department 4320, Chicago, Illinois 60673. It is also available in some university and public libraries or can be ordered by those institutions.

In addition to individual bank data, the Federal Financial

Figure 3-1
First Page of Uniform Bank Performance Report

CERT # 99999 DSB # 99999999   XXXXXXXXXXXXXXXXXX(BANK NAME)XXXXXXXXXXXXXXXXXXXXXXXX XXXXXXXXXXXXX(CITY)XXXXXXXXXXXXXX
CHARTER # 99999

XXXXXXXXX, 19YY UNIFORM BANK PERFORMANCE REPORT

| INFORMATION | SECTIONS | TABLE OF CONTENTS | PAGE NUMBER |

SUMMARY RATIOS....................................01

INCOME INFORMATION:

INCOME STATEMENT – REVENUES AND EXPENSES ($000).........02
NON-INTEREST INCOME AND EXPENSES ($000) AND YIELDS.......03

BALANCE SHEET INFORMATION:

BALANCE SHEET – ASSETS, LIABILITIES & CAPITAL ($000)....04
COMMITMENTS AND CONTINGENCIES.........................05
BALANCE SHEET – % COMPOSITION OF ASSETS & LIABILITIES...06
ANALYSIS OF LOAN & LEASE LOSS RESERVE AND LOAN MIX......07
ANALYSIS OF PAST DUE, NONACCRUAL & RESTRUCTURED LN&LS....08
MATURITY AND REPRICING DISTRIBUTION....................09
LIQUIDITY AND INVESTMENT PORTFOLIOS....................10
CAPITAL ANALYSIS......................................11

FOR ORDERING ASSISTANCE PHONE: (800) 843-1669
   (IN THE WASHINGTON, DC AREA: (202) 898-7108)

QUESTIONS REGARDING CONTENT OF REPORTS: (202) 357-0111

BANK AND BANK HOLDING COMPANY INFORMATION

CERTIFICATE # 99999 BANK # 999999 CHARTER # 999999

XXXXXXXXXXXXXXXXXXXXXXXXXXXXXXXXX
(HOLDING CO. # 99999)   XX
XXXXXXXXXXXXXXXXXXXXXXXXX

INTRODUCTION

THIS UNIFORM BANK PERFORMANCE REPORT COVERS THE OPERATIONS OF YOUR BANK AND THAT OF A COMPARABLE GROUP OF PEER BANKS. IT IS PROVIDED FOR YOUR USE AS A MANAGEMENT TOOL BY THE FEDERAL FINANCIAL INSTITUTIONS EXAMINATION COUNCIL. DETAILED INFORMATION CONCERNING THIS REPORT IS PROVIDED IN " A USER'S GUIDE FOR THE UNIFORM BANK PERFORMANCE REPORT " FORWARDED TO YOUR BANK UNDER SEPARATE COVER. ADDITIONAL COPIES OF THE USER'S GUIDE CAN BE OBTAINED USING THE 'ORDERING INSTRUCTIONS AND ORDER BLANK' ATTACHED TO THIS REPORT.

AS OF THE DATE OF PREPARATION OF THIS REPORT, YOUR BANK'S FEDERAL REGULATOR WAS THE XXXXXXXXXXXXXXXXXXXXXXXXXXXXXXXXXXXX

YOUR CURRENT PEER GROUP # 99
INCLUDES ALL INSURED COMMERCIAL BANKS HAVING ASSETS
XXXXXXXXXXXXXXXXXXXXXXXXXXXXXXXXXXXXXXXXXXXXXXXXXXX
XXXXXXXXXXXXXXXXXXXXXXXXXXXXXXXXXXXXXXXXXXXXXXXXXXX

FOR THE DEFINITION OF OTHER UBPR PEER GROUPS, REFER TO THE UBPR USER'S GUIDE.

ADDRESSEE

CHIEF EXECUTIVE OFFICER
XXXXXXXXXXXXXXXXXXX(BANK NAME)XXXXXXXXXXXXXXXXXXX
XXXXXXXXXXXXXXXX(BANK ADDRESS)XXXXXXXXXXXXXXXXXXX
XXXXXXXXXXXXXXX(CITY)XXXXXXXXXXXXXXXXXXXXX
XXXXXXXXXXXXXX   99999

NOTE

THIS REPORT HAS BEEN PRODUCED FOR THE USE OF THE FEDERAL REGULATORS OF FINANCIAL INSTITUTIONS IN CARRYING OUT THEIR SUPERVISORY RESPONSIBILITIES. ALL INFORMATION CONTAINED HEREIN WAS OBTAINED FROM SOURCES DEEMED RELIABLE; HOWEVER NO GUARANTEE IS GIVEN AS TO THE ACCURACY OF THE DATA OR OF THE CALCULATIONS DERIVED THEREFROM. THE DATA AND CALCULATIONS IN THIS REPORT DO NOT INDICATE APPROVAL OR DISAPPROVAL OF ANY PARTICULAR INSTITUTION'S PERFORMANCE AND ARE NOT TO BE CONSTRUED AS A RATING OF ANY INSTITUTION BY FEDERAL BANK REGULATORS. USERS ARE CAUTIONED THAT ANY CONCLUSIONS DRAWN FROM THIS REPORT ARE THEIR OWN AND ARE NOT TO BE ATTRIBUTED TO THE FEDERAL BANK REGULATORS.

THE REPORTS OF CONDITION AND INCOME FOR THIS BANK CONTAIN ADDITIONAL INFORMATION NOT INCLUDED IN THIS PERFORMANCE REPORT, SUCH AS AN OPTIONAL NARRATIVE STATEMENT BY THE BANK.

Institutions Examination Council publishes a State Averages Report for all states, a Peer Group Report for all twenty-five peer groups, and a User's Guide. These documents can also be purchased from the Federal Financial Institutions Examination Council. Data presented in the Uniform Bank Performance Reports, Peer Group Reports, and State Averages are also available in bulk format on magnetic tapes that can be purchased for purposes of analyzing large numbers of banks or groups of banks. Figure 3-2 on pages 69 and 70 shows the ordering instructions and order form from the Uniform Bank Performance Report. (Prices effective January, 1990.)

Because the Uniform Bank Performance Report contains standardized financial statement data for all banks in the U.S. and is available on a timely basis to all potential users, information contained in this document will form the basis of the presentation on bank financial statements for Chapters 3, 4, and 5.[2] Financial ratios and other tools that will be used to evaluate a bank's condition and performance are provided in the Uniform Bank Performance Report. Comparable analytical information can also be developed from any bank's balance sheet and income statement.

This chapter presents a discussion of the two major bank financial statements–the balance sheet and the income statement, including a brief item-by-item discussion of each account on the statements. The statement of cash flows, (formerly called the flow-of-funds or sources and uses of funds statement), is not included in this discussion because it is neither part of the Uniform Bank Performance Report nor an important tool for the analysis of depository institutions. While the line-by-line descriptive approach to each

---

2. The data provided in the Uniform Bank Performance Report and thus the analysis used in this book are for individual banking institutions. It should be pointed out that if an individual bank is part of a holding company, the performance of the holding company may be different from that of the bank. A bank's holding company status is shown on the first page of the Uniform Bank Performance Report (see Figure 3-1).

THE UNIFORM BANK PERFORMANCE REPORT

ORDER FORM

Complete the appropriate columns indicating the UBPR products desired (refer to instructions on the reverse side). Send order form and check (made payable to the: Federal Financial Institutions Examination Council) to: UBPR, Department 4320, Chicago, IL 60673. For additional information on your UBPR order, please call the FDIC Disclosure Group at 1-800-843-1669 (in the Washington, DC area 1-202-898-7108). For questions regarding content of the UBPR products, please call Jon Wisnieski at 1-202-357-0111.

	FOR FDIC USE ONLY!
Completed order should be mailed to:	
	Log Number.....
CONTACT PERSON:	Date Received..
NAME (Bank or Company):	Dollar Amount..
STREET ADDRESS:	Date Entered...
P.O. BOX:	Date Mailed....
CITY: _____ STATE: _____ ZIP: _____	Processed By...
TELEPHONE NUMBER: _____ DATE ORDERED: _____	Requestors ID..

FDIC CERT NUMBER*	Bank Report for Insured Bank Name	City	State	Call Report Date	# of Copies Requested	Unit Cost	Total Cost
						$30.00	$
						$30.00	$
						$30.00	$
						$30.00	$
						$30.00	$
						$30.00	$
						$30.00	$
						$30.00	$
						$30.00	$
						$30.00	$

*Only if FDIC certificate number is available.

	Peer Group Report				$50.00	$
	Peer Group Report				$50.00	$

	State Average Report				$30.00	$
	State Average Report				$30.00	$

Please note: When ordering more than ten bank reports or more than two peer group or state average reports, please attach an additional sheet.

	User's Guide for the Uniform Bank Performance Report		$15.00	$

	TOTAL COST OF YOUR ORDER (AMOUNT ENCLOSED):		$

item in the financial statement is somewhat tedious, it is necessary to have a basic understanding of the financial statement accounts in order to use the information for analysis in Chapters 4 and 5.

Chapter 4 presents and defines key financial ratios and other analytical tools that facilitate the evaluation of a bank's profitability and risk based on the financial statement data.

THE UNIFORM BANK PERFORMANCE REPORTS

YEAR	MARCH July '90*	JUNE Oct '90	SEPTEMBER Jan '91	DECEMBER April '91
1990				
1989	Yes	Yes	Yes	Yes
1988	Yes	Yes	Yes	Yes
1987	Yes	Yes	Yes	Yes
1986	Yes	.	.	.
1985	.	.	.	.
1984	.	.	.	.
1983	.	.	.	.
1982	.	.	.	.
1981	.	.	.	.

UBPR EDITION AVAILABILITY

*FDIC insured savings bank UBPR's are produced for the first time.

UBPR PRICING SCHEDULE

UBPR PRODUCT	PRICE PER COPY
1. Bank Report	$30.00
2. Peer Group Report	$50.00
3. State Average Report	$30.00
4. User's Guide for the UBPR	$15.00
5. Public Disclosure Tapes	$400.00*

*for each data tape

How To Order UBPR Publications
UBPR publications may be purchased through the FDIC Disclosure Group. All requests must be in writing and payment must be included with the order. Orders should be sent to: UBPR, Department 4320, Chicago, IL 60673. Please make certain to remit the exact dollar amount as nominal overpayments are nonrefundable and underpayments will delay shipment of your request. Refunds will only be made in the event of cancellation of an order or product unavailability.

For additional information on your UBPR order, please call the FDIC Disclosure Group at 1-800-843-1669 (in the Washington, DC area 1-202-898-7108).

For questions regarding content of the UBPR products, please call Jon Viznieski at 1-202-357-0111.

Non-Related UBPR Products
For information concerning the Bank Holding Company Performance Reports, call the Federal Reserve Board Publication Unit at 1-202-452-3244. Currently, the federal regulatory agencies do not produce a performance report for the S&L institutions.

General Information
The Uniform Bank Performance Report (UBPR) is an analytical tool created for bank supervisory purposes. In a concise format, it shows the impact of management decisions and economic conditions on a bank's performance and balance-sheet composition and is produced for each insured commercial bank and FDIC insured savings bank (insured Bank) in the United States. The UBPR is computer-generated from the FDIC data base, contains several year's worth of data, and the data is presented in ratio, percentage, and dollar formats.

UBPR Products
1. **Bank Report** - (approximately 12 pages) prepared for each insured Bank in the U.S.

   Page Description
   Table of Contents
   1 Summary Ratios
   2 Income Statement
   3 Noninterest Income & Expenses
   4 Balance Sheet
   5 Composition of Assets & Liabilities
   6 Loan Allowance & Loan Mix
   7 Past Due, Nonaccrual & Restructured Loans
   8 Maturity & Repricing Distribution
   10 Liquidity & Investment Portfolio
   11 Capital Analysis

2. **Peer Group Report** - (approximately 250 pages) contains eight pages of ratio averages for each UBPR Peer Group as well as national averages. For UBPR comparisons, commercial banks and FDIC insured savings banks are not commingled.

   Page Description
   Table of Contents
   1 Summary Ratios
   2 Overhead, Yield & Cost Ratios
   3 Composition of Assets & Liabilities
   4 Loan Allowance & Loan Mix
   5 Past Due, Nonaccrual & Restructured Loans
   6 Maturity & Repricing Distribution
   7 Investment Portfolio & Capital Analysis
   8 Commitments and Contingencies

3. **State Average Report** - (approximately 75 pages) contains one page of Summary Ratio averages (in the same format as page 1 of the Bank Report) for the nation and each individual state.

4. **User's Guide for the UBPR** - (approximately 100 pages) documents the Bank Report. The User's Guide includes:
   o General and technical UBPR information
   o A sample of each UBPR page and a description of each line item
   o A worksheet for calculating tax-equivalency adjustment.

5. **Public Disclosure Tapes** - data printed on the Bank Report hard copies are available on tape in bulk format for all banks, peer groups and state averages. These tapes may be of use to requestors who wish to select or analyze data for large numbers of banks or peer groups. A typical UBPR edition would include a maximum of: eight unique tapes for bank data, eight unique tapes for bank rank data, and one tape for peer group and state average data.

Data Formats
The typical UBPR format consists of the following:
o **Year-End** - Five consecutive year-end periods (e.g., December 1985 through December 1989).
o **Non-Year-End** - Current period, one-year ago from the current period, and third year-end periods (i.e., March 1990, March 1989, December 1989, December 1988 and December 1987).

Data Types
The typical UBPR Publication presents three types of data for each of five periods:
o **Bank-Level Ratio and Dollar Values:** The source of all bank financial data in all of the UBPR publications is the FDIC Call Reports, which are filed on a calendar quarter basis.
o **Peer Group Averages:** The UBPR system classifies insured commercial banks into 25 unique Peer Groups and FDIC insured savings banks into four unique Peer Groups to show how a group of banks with similar characteristics has performed. This information can be used as a bench mark to assess an individual bank's asset and liability structure, earnings level and off-balance sheet exposure.
o **Bank Percentile Ranks:** Based on the UBPR Peer Groups, the UBPR system ranks each bank ratio within each Peer Group in an ascending order. The resulting percentile rank, ranging from 0 to 99, provides the user an institution's relative position within it's UBPR peer group for each measure.

UBPR Data Availability
Each quarter, approximately 90 days after the Call Report date, each insured bank will automatically receive a copy of its own UBPR Bank Report free of charge. If you have misplaced your bank's UBPR Bank Report an additional copy may be purchased (through the FDIC Disclosure Group). In addition, you may also purchase the UBPR product for your competitors or any other UBPR product by using the order form on the back side of this page.

In Chapter 5 the reader is taken step-by-step through the actual analysis of bank financial statements using the balance sheet and income statement information discussed in Chapter 3 and the analytical tools developed in Chapter 4. Application of the techniques is illustrated through an analysis of two banks, one a large urban bank, the other a small rural bank. The steps illustrated in Chapter 5 enable the reader to analyze the condition and performance of any commercial banking institution, using the Uniform Bank Performance Report or developing comparable ratios from a bank's balance sheet and income statement.

Hundreds of pieces of information in the form of dollar amounts, percentages, and ratios are available in the Uniform Bank Performance Report. Chapters three through five help the user to select and highlight factors in this myriad of information that are most useful in assessing a bank's risk and profitability. This approach should help bank managers and officers to review their institution's condition and performance for any reporting period, over time, and in relation to competitors. The presentation should also be valuable to external analysts who evaluate banking institutions for investment, credit, and other purposes.

The Balance Sheet

A bank's balance sheet presents the institution's financial condition at a single point in time. Balance sheets are prepared on a particular date–usually the last day of a month, a year, or a quarter. Thus the amounts presented on a balance sheet on December 31 might be different from the same amounts on December 30 or January 1. Because balance sheets capture a condition at one time, it is useful to compare data for several accounting periods. Each Uniform Bank Performance Report provides data for five accounting periods.

The balance sheet presents a summary, in dollar amounts, of a bank's assets, liabilities, and capital. Assets represent what the bank owns, primarily loans and investments; liabilities are what the bank owes, principally customer deposits; and the capital (equity) accounts reflect the ownership interest in the bank. By definition, the balance sheet must balance, that is the total of assets must equal the sum of liabilities and capital (equity):

Assets = Liabilities + Capital (Equity).

Table 3-1 shows the balance sheet format that is used in the Uniform Bank Performance Report. The numbers in parenthesis to the left of each account have been added to facilitate discussion in the chapter.

Assets. Loans, the least liquid of banking assets and the major source of risk, comprise the major asset category for most banking institutions as well as the primary source of bank earnings. Lease-financing arrangements substitute for loans in certain types of transactions and are also included in this first section of the balance sheet. (See Table 3-1.) Loans and leases are separately classified by the following categories:

(1) domestic loans secured by real estate;

(2) domestic commercial and industrial loans, including loans to depository institutions, acceptances of other banks, and obligations (other than securities) of states and political subdivisions;

(3) domestic loans to individuals for household, family and other personal expenditures;

(4) domestic loans to finance agricultural production;

(5) all other domestic loans and lease-financing receivables; and

(6) all loans and leases in foreign offices.

From (7) gross loans and leases, the total of categories (1)-(6) above, two deductions are made—(8) unearned income and (9) the total of loan and lease loss reserves—to arrive at (10) net loans and leases.

(8) Unearned income represents the amount of income that has been deducted from a loan, for example in the case of a discounted note, but has not yet been recognized as income on the income statement because it is distributed

Table 3-1
FARMERS' STATE BANK
BALANCE SHEET
Assets, Liabilities, and Capital ($000) at December 31,

Assets:		19x9	19X8	19X7	19X6	19X5
(1)	Real Estate Loans	50393	38975	36539	31232	31710
(2)	Commercial Loans	9615	11381	12956	15247	20218
(3)	Individual Loans	8824	10640	15970	15299	12814
(4)	Agricultural Loans	20680	19654	20602	23066	21848
(5)	Other LN & LS–Domestic	3684	4025	3134	3976	4791
(6)	LN & LS–Foreign	0	0	0	0	0
(7)	Gross Loans & Leases	93196	84675	89201	88820	91381
(8)	Less: Unearned Income	89	282	736	949	913
(9)	Reserves	3006	2536	1247	679	440
(10)	Net Loans & Leases	90101	81857	87218	87192	90028
(11)	U.S. Treas & Agen Securities	54082	44848	31556	39213	34007
(12)	Municipal Securities	32789	34616	41632	27123	29817
(13)	Foreign Debt Securities	0	0	0	0	0
(14)	All Other Securities	0	0	25	25	0
(15)	Int-Bearing Bank Bal.	0	1000	0	0	3850
(16)	Fed Funds Sold & Resales	10500	1500	0	2500	10200
(17)	Trading Account Assets	0	0	0	0	0
(18)	Total Investments	97371	81964	73213	68861	77874
(19)	Total Earning Assets	187472	163821	160431	156053	167902
(20)	Non-Int Cash, Due Fr Banks	9039	10522	8924	10078	6412
(21)	Acceptances	0	0	0	0	0
(22)	Prem, Fx Assets, Cap Leases	2229	2398	2489	2633	2714
(23)	Other Real Estate Owned	2282	3012	3102	2762	30
(24)	Inv. Uncon. Subsidiaries	0	0	0	0	0
(25)	Other Assets	4951	4014	3866	3986	4188
(26)	Total Assets	205973	183767	178812	175512	181246
(27)	Avg. Assets During Qtr.	200462	180049	171811	173445	177615
Liabilities & Capital:						
(28)	Demand Deposits	23063	22528	25322	23555	23954
(29)	All NOW & ATS Accounts	6021	5322	4659	4262	3453
(30)	MMDA Accounts	41402	49797	31323	26575	32175
(31)	Other Savings Deposits	3097	2992	3287	3956	3751
(32)	Nonbrok. Time Deps <$100M	31707	28954	26704	27508	43710
(33)	Core Deposits	105290	109593	91295	85856	107043
(34)	All Brokered Deposits	0	0	0	0	0
(35)	Nonbrok. Time Deps >$100M	83009	57665	70373	72830	57745
(36)	Deps in Foreign Offices	0	0	0	0	0
(37)	Total Deposits	188299	167258	161668	158686	164788
(38)	Fed Funds Purch & Resale	0	0	800	0	0
(39)	Other Borrowings	0	0	0	0	0
(40)	Volatile Liabilities	83009	57665	71173	72830	57745
(41)	Accept.& Other Liabilities	3546	3101	3627	3996	3517
(42)	Total Liab. (Incl. Mtg)	191845	170359	166095	162682	168305
(43)	Sub.Notes & Deben.	0	0	0	0	0
(44)	All Common & Pfd Capital	14128	13408	12717	12830	12941
(45)	Total Liab. & Capital	205973	183767	178812	175512	181246
Memoranda:						
(46)	Officer, Shholder Ln(#)	3	2	4	4	7
(47)	Officer, Shholder Ln ($)	276	176	387	309	1286
(48)	Direct, Indirect Invest in RE	0	0	0	0	0
(49)	Total Curr. Restruc. Debt	0	0	0	0	0

over the life of the note.

(9) The amount in the reserve account reflects an estimate by bank management of probable charge-offs for uncollectible loans and leases at the balance sheet date. Although the regulatory authorities are involved in the estimation process, bank management ultimately determines the final valuation of the reserve account. Actual losses are deducted from the reserve account, and recoveries are added back to reserves. The adequacy of the valuation reserve will be an important element in the analysis of a bank's risk. The reserve for loan and lease losses is carried in the asset section of the balance sheet as a contra-asset account, but is considered capital and counted as primary capital in meeting a bank's capital requirements.

The next major category of bank assets is investment securities. Investments, with the exception of trading account securities, are carried at cost. Since banks are generally prohibited from owning equity securities, the securities that appear on bank balance sheets are almost entirely debt. Regulations force banks to be lenders rather than investors. These investment securities consist of:

(11) U.S. Treasury securities and U.S. government agencies[3] and corporation obligations, a major portion of which is generally pledged against government deposits;

(12) securities issued by states and political subdivisions in the U.S.;

(13) foreign debt securities;

(14) all other securities, including foreign equity and domestic securities;

(15) interest-bearing balances due from banks;

---

3. Examples of U.S. government agency securities are issues of the Government National Mortgage Association (Ginnie Mae), the Federal National Mortgage Association (Fannie Mae), and the Farm Credit System.

(16) federal funds sold and securities purchased under agreements to resell; and

(17) total assets held in trading accounts, which consist of securities that banks hold for resale and for underwriting municipal issues.

(18) Total investments are equal to the sum of all securities, interest-bearing bank balances, fed funds sold, and trading account assets (items (11)-(17) above).

(19) Total earning assets equal the sum of (10) net loans and leases and (18) total investments.

(20) The next account, cash and due from banks, includes total currency, coin, and non-interest-bearing balances due from depository institutions.

(21) Acceptances[4] are customers' liabilities to the bank on acceptances outstanding.

(22) This item includes all of the bank's premises, furniture, fixtures, other long-lived assets–after depreciation–and capitalized leases. (Most capitalized leases for banks involve sale-and-leaseback arrangements in which the bank "sells" property and leases it back from the buyer. Terms are structured to allow the bank to maintain control over the property. These arrangements are made primarily to generate cash. Capitalized leases are recorded as an asset rather than as a lease, as if the bank still "owns" the property, and as a liability for the indebtedness–see item (41) below.)

(23) Other real estate is any other real estate owned by the bank and usually represents property that has been obtained through collateral foreclosures on problem loans.

(24) Investments in unconsolidated subsidiaries represent the bank's equity investments in companies that are not consolidated subsidiaries (consolidated means that the financial statements of the investor and the investee would be

---

4. Acceptances are time drafts, generally used to finance international trade.

combined) of the reporting institution.

The final asset category (25) is all other assets. This includes intangible assets–assets without physical substance–such as goodwill recognized in business combinations.

(26) Total assets refers to the sum of all assets and equals (45) the total of liabilities and capital.

(27) Average assets are calculated for each reporting date. This figure is useful for analytical purposes because account balances on the balance sheet are reported as of a specific date and thus can vary considerably from period to period.

Liabilities. Bank liabilities consist primarily of the various types of deposit accounts that the institution uses to fund its lending and investing activities.

Depository accounts vary in terms of interest-payments, maturity, check-writing privileges, and insurability.

(28) Demand deposits are transaction accounts that are payable to the depositor on demand and pay no interest.

(29) NOW and ATS accounts represent the total of all transaction accounts, including Super NOWs, less (28) demand deposits. They are accounts that pay interest and permit check-writing but do not include money market deposit accounts.

(30) Money market deposit accounts are savings accounts on which the bank pays market interest, and check-writing is limited to a certain number of checks per month.

The (31) other savings deposits category comprises all savings deposits other than money market deposit accounts and includes regular passbook accounts with no set maturity and overdraft protection plan accounts.

(32) Nonbrokered time deposits under $100 thousand are total nonbrokered time deposits (nonbrokered deposits with a fixed maturity) in amounts of less than $100,000.

(33) Core deposits, the sum of items (28)-(32), are deposits

that are not highly interest-sensitive and are considered stable, e.g. expected to remain on deposit over several accounting periods.

In contrast to core deposits, (40) volatile liabilities consist of liability accounts that are more volatile with respect to fluctuations in both volume and interest-rate sensitivity. These include:

(34) all brokered deposits, those sold through brokers in a transaction normally requiring the bank to pay a commission. Brokered deposits can have important implications for a bank's risk, as discussed in the "liquidity" section of Chapter 5. Volatile liabilities also include

(35) nonbrokered time deposits over $100 thousand, large certificates of deposit that are negotiable in a well-established secondary market;

(36) total deposits in foreign offices, dollar-denominated demand and time deposits issued by a bank subsidiary outside the U.S.;

(38) Federal funds purchased and securities sold under agreements to repurchase; and

(39) other liabilities for borrowed money plus interest-bearing demand notes issued to the U.S. Treasury.

(37) Total deposits are all deposit accounts, the sum of items (28)-(36).

The last liability account is (41) acceptances and other liabilities–the sum of the bank's liability on acceptances executed and outstanding, mortgage indebtedness, liability for capitalized leases (see item (22) above), and all other liabilities, such as taxes, dividends payable, and trade credit. Item (42) is the total of all liability accounts, excluding (43) subordinated notes and debentures, which are long-term debt instruments on which claims are subordinated to claims of depositors.

Capital. (43) Subordinated notes and debentures are actually liabilities but are shown in the capital section because this type of debt has the characteristics of capital in terms of maturity and permanence and can be counted as capital in meeting certain regulatory requirements.

(44) All common and preferred capital is the par value of all common and preferred stock outstanding, surplus or additional paid-in capital (the amount by which the original sale of the stock exceeded par value), undivided profits or retained earnings (all of the institution's earnings since its inception less any dividends paid), capital reserves and cumulative foreign currency adjustments (amounts that arise from the translation of foreign subsidiary financial statements into dollars at the end of an accounting period).

(45) total liabilities and capital is the total of (42) liabilities plus (43) and (44) capital and is equal to (26) total assets.

There are four memoranda items listed on the Uniform Bank Performance Report balance sheet:

Items (46) and (47) are the number and dollar amounts, respectively, of loans to executive officers, principal shareholders, and their related interests. These 'insider loans' are important to the analyst because they may not face the same scrutiny as other loans in terms of credit standards, and such loans have caused bank failures.

(48) Direct and indirect investment in real estate is the amount of real estate that the bank and its consolidated subsidiaries have acquired and hold for investment purposes.

(49) Total current restructured debt refers to the amount of loans and leases that have been restructured to reduce either interest or principal because of deterioration in the financial position of the borrower and are in compliance with the modified terms. This item excludes restructured loans

secured by one to four family residences and restructured loans to individuals for household, family and other personal expenditures.

The Income Statement

The income statement, which shows all major categories of revenue and expenditures, the net profit or loss for the period, and the amount of cash dividends declared, measures a firm's financial performance over a period of time, such as a year or a quarter or a month. The income statement and the balance sheet are integrally related and both should be evaluated when assessing bank performance.

Table 3-2 presents the income statement format from the Uniform Bank Performance Report, with numbers in parenthesis added to identify each item for discussion.

Interest Income. Loans are the largest asset category for most bank balance sheets (see discussion above), and (1) interest and fees on loans are the primary sources of bank income. This category of revenue, which includes all year-to-date interest and fees on loans, is presented first on the income statement. (2) Income from lease financing is year-to-date income derived from lease financing receivables.

It is important for the analyst to realize that income reported on loans and leases is "accrued," meaning that it is recognized over the appropriate time period of the loan rather than when cash is actually received. A bank can recognize this income for at least ninety days before the loan goes on "nonaccrual" status.

The income reported in (1) and (2) is divided into (3) fully taxable and (4) tax-exempt portions. The tax-exempt amount includes year-to-date income on loan obligations of state and political subdivisions, and tax-exempt income from direct lease financing. The fully taxable amount is total interest and fees on loans and income from lease-financing receivables less the tax-exempt income.

Table 3-2
FARMERS' STATE BANK
INCOME STATEMENT
REVENUE AND EXPENSES ($000)
For Period ending December 31,

		19x9	19X8	19X7	19X6	19X5
(1)	Interest & Fees on loans	8931	9192	10251	11323	9647
(2)	Income from lease finc.	0	0	0	0	0
(3)	Fully taxable	8880	9142	10180	11206	NA
(4)	Tax Exempt	51	50	71	117	NA
(5)	Estimated tax benefit	38	21	43	0	NA
(6)	Income on loans & leases (TE)	8969	9213	10294	11323	NA
(7)	U.S.Treas, agency securities	3735	3025	4337	4122	2998
(8)	Tax exempt security income	3097	3571	2058	2277	2964
(9)	Estimated tax benefit	1882	2103	1390	1129	2442
(10)	Other securities income	13	0	1	0	0
(11)	Invest. interest income (TE)	8727	8699	7786	7528	8404
(12)	Int. Fed funds sold,resales	192	83	244	365	407
(13)	Int on due from banks	27	5	0	54	738
(14)	Trading account income	0	0	0	0	0
(15)	Total interest income (TE)	17915	18001	18324	19270	19196
(16)	Interest on foreign deposits	0	0	0	0	0
(17)	Interest on CDs over $100M	3248	2924	3919	4825	4268
(18)	Interest on other deposits	6757	7167	7138	8621	7781
(19)	Int of Fed funds purch/repos	16	59	24	83	0
(20)	Interest borrowed money	0	50	11	18	0
(21)	Int on mortgages & leases	0	0	0	0	0
(22)	Int on sub notes & debentures	0	0	0	0	0
(23)	Total interest expense	10021	10200	11092	13547	12254
(24)	Net interest income (TE)	7894	7801	7232	5723	6942
(25)	Non-interest income	571	577	569	491	483
(26)	Adjusted operating income (TE)	8465	8378	7801	6214	7425
(27)	Overhead expense	3624	3876	3435	2823	2851
(28)	Provision loan/lease loss	1294	3208	1980	1142	241
(29)	Prov. allocated transfer risk	NA	NA	NA	NA	NA
(30)	Pretax operating income (TE)	3547	1294	2386	2249	4333
(31)	Securities gains (losses)	1240	3331	734	209	732
(32)	Pretax net operating inc (TE)	4787	4625	3120	2458	5065
(33)	Applicable income taxes	347	8	0	0	-125
(34)	Current tax equiv adjustments	1920	2125	1433	1129	2442
(35)	Other tax equiv adjustments	0	0	0	0	0
(36)	Applicable income tax (TE)	2267	2133	1433	1129	2317
(37)	Net operating income	2520	2492	1687	1329	2748
(38)	Net extraordinary items	0	0	0	0	0
(39)	Net income	2520	2492	1687	1329	2748
(40)	Cash dividends declared	1800	1800	1800	1440	1800
(41)	Retained earnings	720	692	-113	-111	948
(42)	Memo: net int'l income	0	0	0	0	0

(5) The estimated tax benefit results from having tax-exempt loan and lease-financing income from municipal loans and leases. It is estimated and added to income in order to improve the comparability of interest income among different banks over several time periods. A worksheet is available in the Uniform Bank Performance Report User's Guide explaining how this calculation is made. The items with "TE" on the income statement indicate that the estimated tax benefit has been included.

(6) Income on total loans and leases (TE) is the total of (1) income on loans, (2) income from lease-financing receivables, and (5) the estimated tax benefit.

Investment Income typically provides the next largest category of income for banking institutions. (7) U.S. Treasury and agency securities income includes interest on U.S. Treasury securities, other U.S. government agencies and corporate obligations. (8) Interest on municipal securities is interest on securities issued by state and political subdivisions in the U.S. Like loans to municipalities, there is a tax benefit resulting from such investments, shown in (9) estimated tax benefit. (10) Other securities income includes interest on other bonds, notes, debentures and dividends on stock investments. Banks cannot generally own corporate stock as an investment but can hold stock if it is acquired as collateral on loans.

(11) Investment interest income (TE) is the total of items (7), (8), (9), and (10).

Other interest income includes (12) income on federal funds sold and securities purchased under agreements to resell, (13) interest on balances due from banks, and (14) income on assets held in trading accounts (excluding gains, losses, commissions, and fees).

(15) Total interest income (TE) is the sum of (6) income on loans and leases, (11) investment interest income, and interest on items (12), (13), and (14).

Interest expense is the largest expense for most banks. The Uniform Bank Performance Report income statement allocates interest expense in seven categories: (16) interest expense on deposits held in foreign offices; (17) interest paid on time deposits of $100,000 or more; (18) interest on all time deposits except those included in (16) and (17); (19) interest expense on federal funds purchased and securities sold under agreements to repurchase; (20) interest on note balances issued to the U.S. Treasury and on other borrowed money; (21) interest on mortgage debt and capital leases on bank premises, fixed assets, and other real estate owned; and (22) interest on subordinated notes and debentures. (23) Total interest expense is the sum of items (16) through (22).

(24) Net interest income on a tax equivalent basis is (15) total interest income less (23) total interest expense. The relationship between net interest expense–the amount by which interest received exceeds interest paid–and total assets will be an important analytical tool in assessing a bank's ability to generate profits through the management of interest earning assets and interest bearing liabilities.

Other income. (25) Non-interest income includes all other sources of income: from fiduciary activities, service charges on deposits, gains or losses and commissions and fees on assets held in trading accounts, foreign-exchange trading gains or losses, and other foreign transactions. These categories of income have increased in relative importance for many banks as a result of deregulation's impact on interest-earning assets/interest-bearing liabilities and the incumbent pricing pressures that have caused banks to seek other income sources.

(26) Adjusted operating income (TE) is the total of (24) net interest income and (25) non-interest income.

Other expense. Three other types of expenses are deducted from adjusted operating income to arrive at (30) pretax operating income. (27) Overhead expense includes salaries and employee benefits, expenses of premises and fixed assets (net of rental income) and other non-interest operating expenses. (28) The provision for loan and lease losses is the year-to-date amount allocated to loan and lease loss reserves (on the balance sheet). Remember that actual losses are charged against the balance sheet reserves account. See discussion above of balance sheet item (9).

(29) The final "other" expense item is the provision for allocated transfer risk, if applicable.

(31) Gains or losses on the sale, exchange, redemption, or retirement of securities other than those held in trading accounts are netted against (30) pretax operating income to determine (32) pretax operating income on a tax equivalent basis. Security gains and losses can be an important element in measuring bank performance. Until 1983 banks showed these amounts as a separate item after net operating income. In 1983 the S.E.C. issued a requirement that security gains and losses be included in operating income. The analyst should be aware that a bank can influence operating profit for a period through these securities transactions.

Income tax expense. (33) Income tax includes the total estimated federal, state, local and foreign (if applicable) income taxes on operating income (including securities gains and losses). (34) The current tax equivalent adjustment is based on the amount of tax-free income relative to the bank's total pretax income. (35) Other tax-equivalent adjustments include the portion of any tax benefit that results from a tax-loss carryback. These taxes together comprise (36) applicable income taxes (TE).

Net income. (36) Income taxes are deducted from (32) pretax operating income to arrive at (37) net operating income. If there are any (38) extraordinary items, defined as transactions that are both unusual in nature and not expected to recur, these are deducted/added, net of taxes, to determine (39) net income.

Other items. Line (40) shows the total cash dividends declared for the year on all common and preferred stock. (41) Retained earnings are (39) net income for the period less (40) cash dividends declared. There is a final memo item, line (42) that shows net income attributable to international business for banks with foreign offices.

The above discussion has provided a line-by-line description of each account contained in a bank's balance sheet and income statement, according to the format used in the Uniform Bank Performance Report. It is essential to begin an evaluation of bank financial statements with a basic understanding of the information that is presented in the statements. But what do all of the numbers and accounts mean? How can we use the information contained in a financial statement to assess a bank's historical, present, and future performance? These questions will be addressed in the next two chapters.

4

The Tools of Financial Statement Analysis

The objective of any business firm is to maximize return to its owners. In Chapter 2, the mathematical measure of this objective was presented as the relationship between net income and average equity (capital), called the return on equity.

$$\frac{\text{Net Income}}{\text{Average Equity}}$$

To effectively evaluate bank performance the analyst must consider the relationship between risk and return. How much risk can a firm tolerate in order to achieve profit objectives? Risk is a double-edged sword. Increasing risk can improve return on equity–for example, shifting funds from short-term investments in U.S. Treasury securities to the loan portfolio might well enhance the bank's net income for the period by increasing the interest earned, while the capital base remains unchanged. On the other hand, since loans are a riskier use of funds than Treasury notes (the loan may not be repaid, while it is assumed that the U.S. government is good for the cash), the shift could have an opposite-from-desired effect. Increasing the proportion of liabilities relative to capital–through the attraction of foreign depositors for instance–could also improve the return on equity, but the other side of the coin is that the new funding source could be unstable and unpredictable. These simple examples must be multiplied by the hundreds of decisions made by banking managers on a regular basis that affect the risk/return trade off.

The balance sheet and income statement discussed in Chapter 3 provide us with the basis for assessing how well a bank manages the relationship between risk and return. The first section of this chapter discusses bank profitability–how profitable is the bank and why–while the second section focuses on measures of bank risk.

The ratios and other analytical tools presented in this chapter are taken directly from the Uniform Bank Performance Report. As mentioned in Chapter 3, financial statement information on all insured commercial banks in the U.S. is available on a quarterly and annual basis to banks and the general public. The report provides percentage rankings, financial ratios, and peer group averages of major items based on a bank's size and geographic location.

Appendix A to this chapter contains descriptions–by asset size, number of banking officers, and type of location (metropolitan and non-metropolitan)–of the twenty-five peer groups in the Uniform Bank Performance Report. Appendix B provides page samples of the peer group data contained in the Peer Group Report.

The Uniform Bank Performance Report contains many more ratios than will be discussed here. For example, Figure 4-1 presents a complete flow chart of the financial ratios and other data in the Report that relate to a bank's profitability. This chapter provides a specific set of financial ratios that can be used to analyze any bank's profits and risk. The other ratios and material in the Report can be used to enhance the analysis or to focus on specific issues and problems; but the set of ratios presented in the chapter will be a basic one sufficient for most analytical situations. Comparable ratios could also be calculated from a bank's financial statements.

If a bank is a publicly traded institution, the analyst may wish to draw on material presented in its annual report, referring to the notes to the financial statement for additional explanatory information. For the many privately held banks, however, the only financial statement data publicly available is that presented in the Uniform Bank Performance Report. The analytical approach taken in this chapter thus applies to all U.S. insured commercial banks, regardless of size, location, type, or availability of a published shareholders' report.

Using financial ratios. This first section of Chapter 4 covers fifteen key financial ratios, based on balance sheet and income statement numbers, to evaluate a bank's profit performance. The next section presents fifteen measures of bank risk. Financial ratios make it possible to relate various pieces of financial statement data in order to facilitate the interpretation of financial statement numbers. It should be noted, however, that many important aspects of evaluating a bank's performance cannot be quantified in the form of a financial ratio. (These issues will be discussed in Chapter 5.)

Because financial ratios express a mathematical relationship, it is important to review simultaneously the absolute dollar amounts in financial statements along with the percentages calculated in the ratio. For example, assume that the return on assets (net income/average assets) for a bank increased from .01 to .02 between 19X8 and 19X9. This improvement in the return on assets could be the result of increasing profits, a decreasing asset base, or both. It will be necessary to look at the actual balance sheet (average assets) and income statement (net income) amounts used to calculate the ratio in order to explain and interpret the result.

Figure 4-1
Flowchart of Uniform Bank Performance Report
Financial Ratios and Other Data

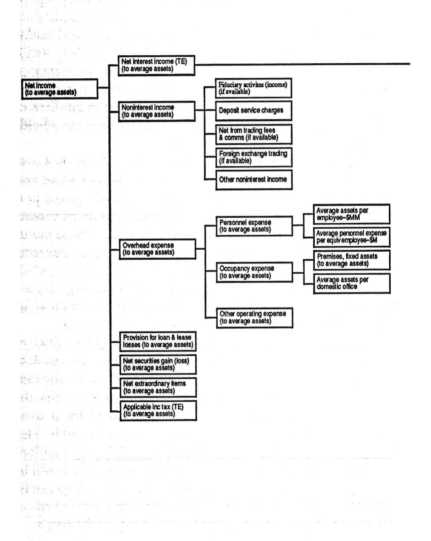

Figure 4-1 (continued)

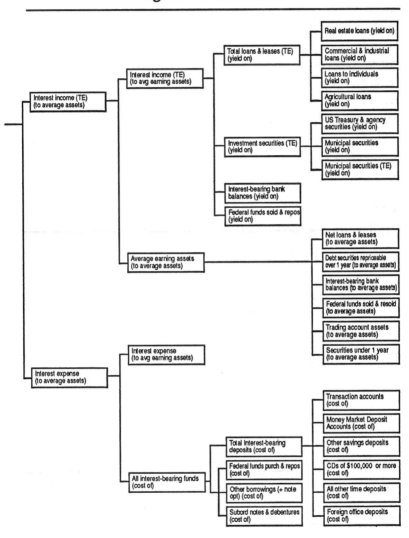

Financial ratios use data from both the balance sheet and the income statement. As discussed, the balance sheet is prepared at a point in time and shows amounts outstanding on a particular date, while the income statement shows the flow of funds over an accounting period. A financial ratio that mixes balance sheet (stock) amounts with income statement (flow) figures should thus use average amounts for the balance sheet figures where possible.

It is essential that the analyst use the financial ratios described in this chapter with a considerable amount of common sense and judgment.

Profitability

The basic equation for evaluating bank performance was presented in Chapter 2:

$$\frac{\text{Net income}}{\text{Average assets}} \times \frac{\text{Average assets}}{\text{Average equity}} = \frac{\text{Net income}}{\text{Average equity}}$$

Return on equity (net income/average equity), the measure of a firm's ability to generate profit relative to owner's capital, is the product of the return on assets, also called return on investment, (net income/average assets), and the leverage multiplier (average assets/average equity). In a simple sense, return on assets is an overall profit measure; the leverage multiplier is a measure of risk; and the return on equity is a summary measure of bank performance. The return to owners is thus the result of profit and risk. In the analysis of bank profitability, the focus will be on the first relationship in the equation: return on assets (net income/average assets).

Figure 4-2 presents a flow chart that shows how the fifteen key financial ratios presented in the section are used to analyze bank profitability.

Figure 4-2
Fifteen Key Financial Ratios

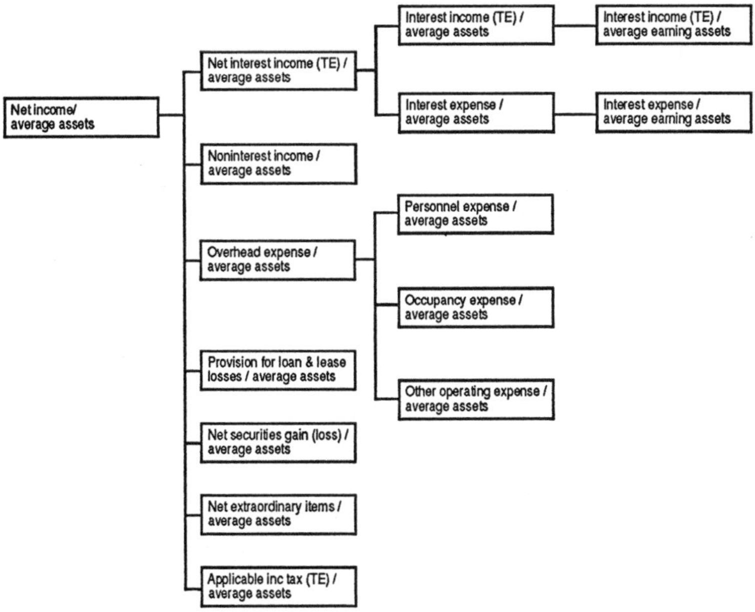

Profitability Ratios

(1) Net income/average assets

(2) Net interest income/average assets

(3) Non-interest income/average assets

(4) Overhead expense/average assets

(5) Provision for loan and lease losses/average assets

(6) Net securities gains or losses/average assets

(7) Net extraordinary items/average assets

(8) Applicable income taxes/average assets

(9) Interest income/average assets

(10) Interest expense/average assets

(11) Interest income/average earning assets

(12) Interest expense/average earning assets

(13) Personnel expense/average assets

(14) Occupancy expense/average assets

(15) Other operating expense/average assets

The first ratio is (1) return on assets (net income/average assets). This ratio tells us how much profit the bank is generating for every dollar invested in assets and is an overall measure of the bank's ability to produce profit from its loans, investments, and other assets.

The major revenues and expenditures that affect net income are net interest income (interest income less interest expense), non-interest income, overhead expense, the provision for loan and lease losses, net securities gains (losses), net extraordinary items, and income taxes. The ratios used to analyze the principal components of net income that impact (1) return on assets, using average assets as the common denominator, are: (2) net interest income/average assets, (3) non- interest income/average assets, (4) overhead expense/ average assets, (5) provision for loan and lease losses/average assets, (6) net securities gains or losses/average assets, (7) net extraordinary items/average assets, and (8) applicable income taxes/average assets. The absolute amount of average assets and how assets are changing over time is an important element in interpreting the ratios. These ratios provide us with perspective on the specific sources of revenue and expense and how these elements change over time, as well as how the bank performs in each area relative to its peers.

In addition to the set of ratios based on primary revenues and expenses, the flow chart adds components that affect specific key areas of revenue and expense. Net interest income is a function of interest income and interest expense, reflected in the ratios (9) interest income/average assets and (10) interest expense/average assets. Extending the analysis further, it is useful to consider the relationship of (11) interest income/average earning assets as well as (12) interest expense/average earning assets since it is earning assets alone that generate interest income. Earning assets are loans and leases (less the reserve for loan losses) and investments in securities.

Overhead expenses consist of personnel expense, occupancy expense, and other operating expenses. Because the control of overhead expense is an important managerial objective in generating profit, the model includes (13) personnel expense/average assets, (14) occupancy expense/average assets, and (15) other operating expense/average assets to help assess any potential problems in managing bank overhead.

These fifteen ratios will provide us with an overview of a bank's historical record in generating profit, the reasons for its success or failure, and how the record has changed over time. The annual data in the Uniform Bank Performance Report enable the analyst to look at each of these ratios over a five-year period and in relation to the bank's peer group. (Quarterly reports also present five periods of data, two partial years and three full years.) For example, the financial statements for the Farmers' State Bank were introduced in Chapter 3 and are repeated here as Tables 4-1 and 4-2. The financial ratios for this bank are also available in its Uniform Bank Performance Report. Chapter 5 will present a complete five-year analysis of Farmer's State.

For now, to illustrate how to use the profitability ratios, let's look at the fifteen key profitability ratios for 19X9 only and the comparable peer group ratios and percentile rankings within the peer group for that period. This information is presented in Table 4-3 with the percentile peer group rankings in parenthesis. The peer group for Farmers' State

Table 4-1
FARMERS' STATE BANK
BALANCE SHEET
Assets, Liabilities, and Capital ($000) at December 31,

Assets:		19x9	19X8	19X7	19X6	19X5
(1)	Real Estate Loans	50393	38975	36539	31232	31710
(2)	Commercial Loans	9615	11381	12956	15247	20218
(3)	Individual Loans	8824	10640	15970	15299	12814
(4)	Agricultural Loans	20680	19654	20602	23066	21848
(5)	Other LN & LS–Domestic	3684	4025	3134	3976	4791
(6)	LN & LS–Foreign	0	0	0	0	0
(7)	Gross Loans & Leases	93196	84675	89201	88820	91381
(8)	Less: Unearned Income	89	282	736	949	913
(9)	Reserves	3006	2536	1247	679	440
(10)	Net Loans & Leases	90101	81857	87218	87192	90028
(11)	U.S. Treas & Agen Securities	54082	44848	31556	39213	34007
(12)	Municipal Securities	32789	34616	41632	27123	29817
(13)	Foreign Debt Securities	0	0	0	0	0
(14)	All Other Securities	0	0	25	25	0
(15)	Int-Bearing Bank Bal.	0	1000	0	0	3850
(16)	Fed Funds Sold & Resales	10500	1500	0	2500	10200
(17)	Trading Account Assets	0	0	0	0	0
(18)	Total Investments	97371	81964	73213	68861	77874
(19)	Total Earning Assets	187472	163821	160431	156053	167902
(20)	Non-Int Cash, Due Fr Banks	9039	10522	8924	10078	6412
(21)	Acceptances	0	0	0	0	0
(22)	Prem, Fx Assets, Cap Leases	2229	2398	2489	2633	2714
(23)	Other Real Estate Owned	2282	3012	3102	2762	30
(24)	Inv. Uncon. Subsidiaries	0	0	0	0	0
(25)	Other Assets	4951	4014	3866	3986	4188
(26)	Total Assets	205973	183767	178812	175512	181246
(27)	Avg. Assets During Qtr.	200462	180049	171811	173445	177615
Liabilities & Capital:						
(28)	Demand Deposits	23063	22528	25322	23555	23954
(29)	All NOW & ATS Accounts	6021	5322	4659	4262	3453
(30)	MMDA Accounts	41402	49797	31323	26575	32175
(31)	Other Savings Deposits	3097	2992	3287	3956	3751
(32)	Nonbrok. Time Deps <$100M	31707	28954	26704	27508	43710
(33)	Core Deposits	105290	109593	91295	85856	107043
(34)	All Brokered Deposits	0	0	0	0	0
(35)	Nonbrok. Time Deps >$100M	83009	57665	70373	72830	57745
(36)	Deps in Foreign Offices	0	0	0	0	0
(37)	Total Deposits	188299	167258	161668	158686	164788
(38)	Fed Funds Purch & Resale	0	0	800	0	0
(39)	Other Borrowings	0	0	0	0	0
(40)	Volatile Liabilities	83009	57665	71173	72830	57745
(41)	Accept.& Other Liabilities	3546	3101	3627	3996	3517
(42)	Total Liab. (Incl. Mtg)	191845	170359	166095	162682	168305
(43)	Sub.Notes & Deben.	0	0	0	0	0
(44)	All Common & Pfd Capital	14128	13408	12717	12830	12941
(45)	Total Liab. & Capital	205973	183767	178812	175512	181246
Memoranda:						
(46)	Officer, Shholder Ln(#)	3	2	4	4	7
(47)	Officer, Shholder Ln ($)	276	176	387	309	1286
(48)	Direct, Indirect Invest in RE	0	0	0	0	0
(49)	Total Curr. Restruc. Debt	0	0	0	0	0

Table 4-2
FARMERS' STATE BANK
INCOME STATEMENT
REVENUE AND EXPENSES ($000)
For Period ending December 31,

		19x9	19X8	19X7	19X6	19X5
(1)	Interest & Fees on loans	8931	9192	10251	11323	9647
(2)	Income from lease finc.	0	0	0	0	0
(3)	Fully taxable	8880	9142	10180	11206	NA
(4)	Tax Exempt	51	50	71	117	NA
(5)	Estimated tax benefit	38	21	43	0	NA
(6)	Income on loans & leases (TE)	8969	9213	10294	11323	NA
(7)	U.S.Treas, agency securities	3735	3025	4337	4122	2998
(8)	Tax exempt security income	3097	3571	2058	2277	2964
(9)	Estimated tax benefit	1882	2103	1390	1129	2442
(10)	Other securities income	13	0	1	0	0
(11)	Invest. interest income (TE)	8727	8699	7786	7528	8404
(12)	Int. Fed funds sold,resales	192	83	244	365	407
(13)	Int on due from banks	27	5	0	54	738
(14)	Trading account income	0	0	0	0	0
(15)	Total interest income (TE)	17915	18001	18324	19270	19196
(16)	Interest on foreign deposits	0	0	0	0	0
(17)	Interest on CDs over $100M	3248	2924	3919	4825	4268
(18)	Interest on other deposits	6757	7167	7138	8621	7781
(19)	Int of Fed funds purch/repos	16	59	24	83	0
(20)	Interest borrowed money	0	50	11	18	0
(21)	Int on mortgages & leases	0	0	0	0	0
(22)	Int on sub notes & debentures	0	0	0	0	0
(23)	Total interest expense	10021	10200	11092	13547	12254
(24)	Net interest income (TE)	7894	7801	7232	5723	6942
(25)	Non-interest income	571	577	569	491	483
(26)	Adjusted operating income (TE)	8465	8378	7801	6214	7425
(27)	Overhead expense	3624	3876	3435	2823	2851
(28)	Provision loan/lease loss	1294	3208	1980	1142	241
(29)	Prov. allocated transfer risk	NA	NA	NA	NA	NA
(30)	Pretax operating income (TE)	3547	1294	2386	2249	4333
(31)	Securities gains (losses)	1240	3331	734	209	732
(32)	Pretax net operating inc (TE)	4787	4625	3120	2458	5065
(33)	Applicable income taxes	347	8	0	0	-125
(34)	Current tax equiv adjustments	1920	2125	1433	1129	2442
(35)	Other tax equiv adjustments	0	0	0	0	0
(36)	Applicable income tax (TE)	2267	2133	1433	1129	2317
(37)	Net operating income	2520	2492	1687	1329	2748
(38)	Net extraordinary items	0	0	0	0	0
(39)	Net income	2520	2492	1687	1329	2748
(40)	Cash dividends declared	1800	1800	1800	1440	1800
(41)	Retained earnings	720	692	-113	-111	948
(42)	Memo: net int'l income	0	0	0	0	0

Table 4-3
Farmers' State Bank Profitability Ratios

Financial Ratio	Farmers' State Bank	Peer Group
(1) Net income/avg. assets	1.31	0.84 (78)
(2) Net interest inc./avg. assets	4.10	3.90 (59)
(3) Non-interest inc./avg. assets	0.30	0.58 (13)
(4) Overhead exp./avg. assets	1.88	2.56 (14)
(5) Prov: ln & ls loss/avg. assets	.67	0.68 (62)
(6) Sec gn or loss/avg. assets	0.64	0.02 (99)
(7) Net ext. items/avg. assets	NA	NA
(8) Appl. inc. tax/avg. assets	1.18	0.64 (88)
(9) Interest inc/avg. assets	9.31	8.88 (71)
(10) Interest exp/avg. assets	5.21	4.99 (67)
(11) Int inc/avg. earn assets	10.01	9.56 (74)
(12) Int exp/avg. earn assets	5.60	5.38 (67)
(13) Pers exp/avg. assets	0.96	1.22 (23)
(14) Occ exp/avg. assets	0.18	0.33 (12)
(15) Other op exp/avg. assets	0.74	0.95 (30)

includes all insured commercial banks having assets between $100 million and $300 million with two or less banking offices, and located in a non-metropolitan area.

The 0.84 (78) peer group ranking for Farmers' State Bank's net income/average assets ratio means that the average peer group ratio of net income/average assets for 19X9 was 0.84 and Farmers' State was in the 78th percentile of the peer group. This indicates that seventy-seven percent of the banks in the peer group had a lower net income/average assets ratio. Figure 4-3 shows the same information in flow chart format.

We now have a capsule of Farmers' State Bank's profit generation for 19X9. (Due to rounding in the financial state-

Figure 4-3
Flowchart of Key Financial Ratios
(with percentile peer group rankings)

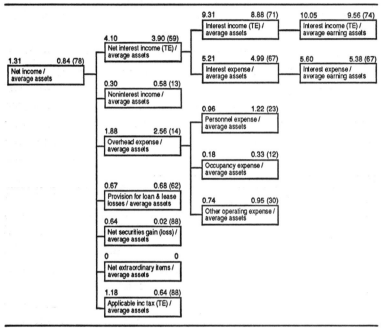

ment data presented in the Uniform Bank Performance Report, the actual ratio calculations in the Report are slightly different from those that would be calculated from the financial statement numbers shown.)

As seen in the ratios, the bank was more profitable than its peer group (1) with an overall return on assets of 1.31 compared with .84 for the peer group. Farmers' State ranked seventy-eight percent in the peer group or in the top quarter. What accounted for the better-than-peer 19X9 performance? Higher relative (2) net interest income, lower (4) overhead expenses, and (6) gains on sales of securities were the primary factors. Farmers' State had (2) net interest income/

average assets of 4.10 compared with 3.90 for the peer group, indicating a better than average ability to manage interest earning assets relative to interest bearing liabilities. Looking at ratios (9), (10), (11), and (12)Farmers' State had higher interest costs than its peers, but the income earned more than offset the higher interest expense.

Farmers' State's (3) non-interest income/average assets were actually less than its peer group–0.30 compared with the peer groups' 0.58. Non-interest income, however, is a less significant proportion of total income than interest income. Farmers' State also had lower (4) overhead expenses relative to assets than the peer group–1.88 compared with 2.56, and the lower expenses applied to all three categories: (13) personnel, (14) occupancy and (15) other operating expense.

Farmers' State ranked in the ninety-ninth percentile relative to its peers in gains from securities' sales/average assets. Remember that securities gains and losses can fluctuate considerably from period to period (see Farmers' State Banks' Income Statement in Table 4-2) and, to a considerable extent, are a function of management's discretion.

It should be noted that Farmers' State's (5) loan and lease loss provision/average assets ratio was almost identical to the peer group's. One of the ratios that we will look at in the examination of a bank's liquidity later in the chapter is the proportion of loans and leases to assets. If Farmers' State has loss provision/assets that equal the peer group, a logical next step is to relate this provision to the proportion of loans and leases. To look ahead, Farmers' State's percentage of loans and leases/assets in 19X9 is 43.74 percent, lower than the peer group's 48.70 percent. If the loan loss provision is average, and the loan portfolio is less than the average, it could mean that Farmers' State has a riskier portfolio and/or uses a more conservative approach to the loan/loss provision.

Finally, Farmers' State had no (7) extraordinary items (banks rarely do) and the (8) applicable income taxes/average assets were higher than the peer group's, primarily because its profits were greater. A full understanding of the 19X9 profits for Farmers' State will require looking at 19X9 in an historical context over a five year period, which will be part of the Chapter 5 analysis.

Risk

The assessment of bank risk is the second essential element in the process of evaluating bank performance. Unfortunately, however, there is no set of financial statement data, ratios, and/or other analytical tools that can be used to assess risk with complete accuracy. If risk-evaluation were a clearcut process, there would be fewer bank failures. In this section a combination of financial ratios and growth rates that provides an overview of the nature and degree of risk inherent in an institution's financial statement record is discussed. To the extent possible, this historical record of strengths and weaknesses is used to assess the future. The measures of bank risk presented in this section correspond to the discussion of risk introduced in Chapter 2 and focus on a bank's overall risk as well as the following key areas: credit risk, liquidity, interest rate risk, and fraud risk.

Measures of Bank Risk

Overall risk:
(16) Primary capital/adjusted average assets
(17) Growth rate: assets
(18) Growth rate: primary capital
(19) Cash dividends/net operating income

Credit risk:
  (20) Net loss/total loans and leases
  (21) Earnings coverage of net loss (X)
  (22) Loss reserve/net loss (X)
  (23) Loss reserve/total loans and leases
  (24) Percent noncurrent loans and leases
   (5) Provision loan loss/average assets
Liquidity:
  (25) Temporary investments/volatile liabilities
  (26) Volatile liability dependence
  (27) Loans and leases/assets
Interest rate:
  (28) Gap
Fraud risk:
  (29) Officer, shareholder loans/assets
Summary
  (30) Net income/average equity

  Capital Risk. To measure overall risk or capital risk it is necessary to consider the relationship between assets and capital. In general, the larger the capital base in proportion to assets, the less overall riskiness. To begin the analysis of risk we will use the ratio (16) primary capital/adjusted average assets. The Uniform Bank Performance Report does not provide the ratio, introduced in Chapter 2, of average equity/average assets or average assets/average equity. Rather, the report narrows the definition of capital to primary capital, considered the most important part of total capital and includes this ratio of primary capital to adjusted average assets. Primary capital includes common equity, the loan and lease loss reserve, permanent and convertible preferred stock, qualifying mandatory convertible debt, and minority interest in consolidated subsidiaries, less intangible assets. (Secondary capital is limited to a maximum of fifty percent of primary capital and includes limited life preferred stock and qualifying subordinated debt). Adjusted average assets are average assets for the current quarter when reported, or period-ending total assets, plus the loan and lease loss reserve, less total intangible assets, plus intangible assets qualifying as primary capital.

Because of the important relationship between assets and capital in measuring a bank's overall risk, it is useful to consider (17) the growth rate of assets and (18) the growth rate of primary capital. If a bank is growing too fast, as measured by the growth rate of assets, there is a greater potential for risk since such growth typically comes from lower quality loans. Core deposits grow at fairly predictable rates, so new funding sources may be unstable. Risk could be reduced by a proportionate growth in capital. A capital base that is increasing faster than assets would be interpreted as risk-reduction. In each case the analyst needs to consider the reasons for growth.

It is important to remember that risk is not bad; increasing risk can multiply the return to shareholders. At issue is risk-management–risk that is within the dimensions and management capabilities of the banking institution, considering its operating environment.

Another measure of capital risk is (19) cash dividends/net operating income. As mentioned above, the higher the proportion of capital relative to assets, the lower the degree of overall risk. The relationship between dividends and income (the dividend payout ratio) provides information about how much capital is left–after payments to shareholders–for the firm's growth. Thus the higher the dividend payout ratio, the lower the potential for internal capital growth.

Credit Risk is a major cause of bank failures and thus a key element in the assessment of bank risk. There are many pieces of information in the Uniform Bank Performance Report and any bank's financial statements relating to credit risk. Six key ratios are identified here for use in the analysis of credit risk but this is by no means an exhaustive list. These ratios will, however, enable the analyst to evaluate the main variables affecting credit risk.

(20) Net loss/total loans and leases are determined by gross loan and lease charge-offs, less gross recoveries, divided by average total loans and leases. This ratio shows the proportion of the bank's portfolio that has resulted in losses during the accounting period.

(21) Earnings coverage of net loss (X) is net operating income before taxes, securities gains or losses, and extraordinary items, plus the provision for loans and lease losses, divided by net loan and lease losses. The "X" indicates that this ratio is expressed in "times," the number of times earnings cover losses. Here we are looking at the stability of earnings relative to loan and lease losses.

(22) Loss reserve to net loss (X) is the ending balance of the allowance for possible loan and lease losses divided by net loan and lease losses. This ratio considers the relationship between management's estimates of loan/lease losses and the actual write-offs.

(23) Loss reserve to total loans and leases represents the ending balance of the allowance for loan and lease losses divided by total loans and leases and provides perspective on the relationship between the allowance for bad loans relative to the total portfolio.

(24) Percent of noncurrent loans and leases is the sum of loans and leases past due at least ninety days, plus those in nonaccrual status, divided by gross loans and leases outstanding. This ratio looks at potential losses relative to total loans and leases.

In addition, the analyst would want to consider, from the profitability analysis section above, (5) the provision for loan and lease losses/average assets as a measure of estimated losses relative to total investment in assets.

Liquidity. Liquidity ratios measure the ability of a firm to meet cash needs as they arise, with a minimum of loss. It is obvious that failure to meet such claims can be disastrous. Both assets and liabilities are used as sources of liquidity with smaller banks more likely to rely on short-term assets and larger banks leaning more heavily on liabilities. Three measures of banking liquidity are focused on here: (25) temporary investments/volatile liabilities, (26) the volatile liability dependence ratio, and (27) total loans and leases/ assets.

(25) Temporary investments/volatile liabilities shows the relationship between a bank's most liquid assets and the liabilities which fluctuate the greatest in terms of volume and interest rate sensitivity—its most predictable, relative to its least predictable, sources of funds. The higher this ratio, the greater the bank's liquidity. Temporary investments include fed funds sold, trading account assets, investment securities with maturities of one year or less and due from banks. Volatile liabilities are brokered deposits, jumbo CD's, deposits in foreign offices, fed funds purchased and resold, and other borrowings. Brokered deposits are a particularly important part of volatile liabilities because banks that are experiencing liquidity problems often resort to brokered deposits as their last source of funds.

(26) The volatile liability dependence ratio is somewhat complicated but extremely useful in measuring liquidity. The ratio is calculated as volatile liabilities less temporary investments divided by the sum of net loans and leases and debt securities over one year. It considers the degree to which

the riskiest assets (loans, lease-financing, and long-term security investments) are being funded by unstable or "hot" money, funds that can disappear from the bank overnight. The volatile liability dependence ratio varies inversely with liquidity.

(27) Loans and lease-financing arrangements are the least liquid assets that banks hold as well as the greatest source of potential losses. Net loans and leases/assets looks at the proportion of a bank's assets that is accounted for by the least liquid funding source. In general, the higher this ratio, the lower the overall liquidity, but the analyst would want to consider the composition of the loan portfolio and how that is changing over time when interpreting the ratio.

Interest Rate Risk can only be approximated from information provided in the current format of the Uniform Bank Performance Report. If a bank had no interest rate risk, profit would not be affected by movements in interest rates. The interest rate gap is the most widely used measure of interest rate risk, reflecting the effect changes in interest rate have on bank profitability. If profits are affected by changes in interest rates, the bank either holds more interest rate sensitive assets than liabilities or the reverse. When more interest rate sensitive liabilities are held during a period of rising interest rates, profitability will be impaired because the bank will face higher pay-out costs than it is receiving in increased interest receipts. During a period of declining interest rates, profitability will be lessened if the bank holds more interest sensitive assets than liabilities.

The difference between rate sensitive assets and rate sensitive liabilities, referred to as "the gap," (expressed in either dollar or percentage terms) can be estimated from the Uniform Bank Performance Report data that show the maturity and repricing distribution of assets and liabilities at the end of the accounting period for which the report is prepared. If the gap is positive, the bank holds more interest rate sensitive assets than liabilities. A negative gap means that there are more rate sensitive liabilities than assets.

Figure 4-4 shows the information needed to estimate Farmers' State Bank's (28) interest rate gap as of December 31, 19X9. The data presented in Exhibit 4-4 is a portion of page nine, "Maturity and Repricing Distribution," of the Uniform Bank Performance Report. In the three-month period ending December 31, 19X9, 25.39 percent of Farmers' State's assets consist of interest-bearing assets that reprice within three months, and 43.65 percent are interest bearing liabilities that reprice within three months. The net position is -18.25 percent, a negative gap indicating that the bank's profits will rise if interest rates fall and decline if interest rates rise. Farmers' State's peer group had a negative gap of -6.25, and Farmers' State was in the seventeenth percentile of banks in the group.

Fraud Risk. While fraud risk is a major cause of bank failure, it is, as pointed out earlier in this book, extremely difficult to detect. The Uniform Bank Performance Report provides data on the number and amount of loans to insiders –officers and shareholders. It also provides the ratio of (29) officer and shareholder loans to total assets, which is the only ratio presented that is relevant to fraud risk, at least from insider loans. (There are obviously many other avenues for fraud that cannot be measured from the bank's financial statements.)

Summary. The final measure of bank performance is the return on equity, (30) net income/total average equity. This ratio provides an overall measure of the bank's ability to manage risk and maximize profit generation for its owners.

For Farmers' State Bank, Table 4-4 shows the measures of

Figure 4-4

FARMERS' STATE BANK
MATURITY AND REPRICING DISTRIBUTION
AS OF 12/31/X9

Cumulative Amount as a Percent of Assets

		Percent Repriced Within 3 Months	
ASSETS	Bank	Peer	Pct
LOANS AND LEASES (EXCL NONACC)	16.14	28.11	19
FIXED RATE BY MATURITY	4.82	4.78	62
FLOATING RATE BY REP INTERVAL	11.32	22.93	22
DEBT SECURITIES	1.43	2.37	44
FIXED RATE BY MATURITY	1.43	1.64	55
FLOATING RATE BY REP INTERVAL	0.00	0.18	65
FEDERAL FUNDS SOLD (OVERNIGHT)*	7.82	3.69	85
SECURITIES PURCHASED UNDER			
AGREEMENT TO RESELL*	0.00	0.00	96
INTEREST-BEARING BANK BALANCES*			
TRADING ACCOUNT ASSETS*	0.00	0.00	97
TOTAL INT-BEARING ASSETS (IBA)	25.39	35.11	26
LIABILITIES			
DEPOSITS IN FOREIGN OFFICES**			
CD'S OF $100,000 OR MORE	5.26	6.63	48
FIXED RATE BY MATURITY	5.26	6.51	49
FLOATING RATE BY REP INTERVAL	0.00	0.00	89
OTHER TIME DEPOSITS	14.81	8.82	91
MONEY MARKET DEPOSIT ACCOUNTS*	11.89	13.67	42
OTHER SAVINGS DEP (EXCL MMDA)**			
NOW ACCOUNTS*	11.12	9.66	68
FEDERAL FUNDS PURCH (OVERNIGHT)*	0.00	0.04	71
SECURITIES SOLD UNDER			
AGREEMENT TO REPURCHASE*	0.00	0.92	50
OTHER BORROWED MONEY*			
SUB NOTES & DEBENTURES**			
TREASURY NOTES*	0.57	0.18	88
TOTAL INT-BEARING LIABS (IBL)	43.65	41.27	62
NET POSITION (IBA - IBL)	-18.25	-6.25	17

*INDICATES ITEMS THAT ARE NOT REPORTED BY MATURITY/REPRICING INTER-
VAL, HOWEVER, REPRICING ASSUMPTIONS WERE MADE.
**INDICATES ITEMS THAT ARE NOT REPORTED BY MATURITY/REPRICING INTER-
VAL, HOWEVER, NO REPRICING ASSUMPTIONS WERE MADE.

bank risk that have been discussed for 19X9 and the comparable peer group averages and percentile ranking within the peer group in parenthesis.

In terms of overall or capital risk in 19X9, the growth rate of assets and primary capital indicate more risk for Farmers' State than its peer group. Assets grew much faster in 19X9 and capital did not keep pace. The balance sheet for Farmers' State in Table 4-1 reveals that much of the increase in assets stemmed from growth in real estate loans, which typically carry a relatively high degree of risk. The primary capital/ assets for Farmers' State are about average relative to the peer group, but Farmers' State is paying out a much greater proportion of its income in cash dividends, thereby limiting the potential for internal capital growth.

Credit risk measures show that Farmer's State's net losses on loans and leases, earnings coverage of net losses, and the loss provision/assets in 19X9 were about comparable to its peers with a percentile ranking of fifty-one, fifty, and fifty-nine, respectively. The credit risk ratio that stands out for Farmers' State in 19X9 is the loss reserve to total loans and leases. The fact that Farmers' State ranks in the ninetieth percentile could mean that the bank has more credit risk relative to its peers–perhaps because of the large increase in real estate loans in 19X9. Or, Farmers' may be taking a more conservative approach to the loss reserve, as indicated by the fact that the bank's times coverage of net losses is higher than its peer group while the percentage of noncurrent loans is less. The five-year analysis of Farmers' State in Chapter 5 will help put these ratios in historical context.

Table 4-4
Measures of Bank Risk

Financial Ratio	FSB	Peer Group
Overall risk:		
(16) Primary capital/adj. avg. assets	8.42	8.85 (45)
(17) Growth rate–assets	12.08	3.51 (83)
(18) Growth rate–primary capital	7.46	5.98 (53)
(19) Cash div/net operating income	71.43	45.75 (71)
Credit risk:		
(20) Net loss/total loans & leases	0.92	1.18 (51)
(21) Earn coverage of net loss (X)	3.54	6.02 (50)
(22) Loss reserve/net loss (X)	3.65	2.54 (73)
(23) Loss reserve/tot. loans & leases	3.23	1.92 (90)
(24) Percent noncurrent loans & leases	2.44	3.00 (NA)
(5) Provision loan loss/avg. assets	0.67	0.68 (59)
Liquidity:		
(25) Temporary invest/volatile liab.	15.25	43.50 (04)
(26) Volatile liability dependence	40.24	-5.41 (97)
(27) Loans & leases/assets	43.74	48.70 (38)
Interest rate:		
(28) Gap	-18.25	-6.25 (17)
Fraud risk:		
(29) Officer, shareholder loans/assets	0.13	0.18 (54)
Summary:		
(30) Net income/average equity	25.98	11.10 (97)

Farmers' State would appear to have considerable liquidity risk in 19X9. Although loans and leases as a percent of assets are somewhat lower than the peer group, temporary investments to volatile liabilities are much lower and the volatile liability dependence ratio is considerably higher. These measures of liquidity suggest that Farmers' State is far more dependent than its peers on volatile liabilities as a funding source, and this money could leave the bank overnight.

Farmers' State had a negative gap, which means that the bank has more interest rate sensitive liabilities than assets at the end of 19X9. Because 19X9 was a year of falling interest rates, this negative gap worked to Farmers' State's advantage by contributing positively to profit margins. On the other hand, the bank runs the risk of losses if interest rates increase unless it can make a short-run shift to a positive gap.

There is no apparent potential for fraud risk from insider loans at Farmers' State at the end of 19X9.

Farmers' State, overall, performed considerably better than its peers in 19X9, as measured by the return on equity. It ranked very near the top of its peer group (ninety-seventh percentile), and the return on equity at 25.98 was more than double the peer group average. The bank's better-than-peer 19X9 performance was the combined result of higher profits –particularly from net interest income and securities gains– and greater risk, especially in the areas of asset growth, liquidity risk, and the management of interest rate sensitive assets and liabilities.

A bank's overall performance for any one accounting period is important not only in relation to its peers–but in how it has functioned over time in the key areas discussed in this chapter. Chapter 5 will consider a five-year analysis of Farmers' State.

APPENDIX A – PEER GROUP DESCRIPTIONS

INCLUDES ALL INSURED COMMERCIAL BANKS WITH THE FOLLOWING CHARACTERISTICS:

PEER GROUP NUMBER	ASSETS*	NUMBER OF BANKING OFFICES	LOCATION**
1	IN EXCESS OF $10 BILLION	-	-
2	BETWEEN $3 BILLION AND $10 BILLION	-	-
3	BETWEEN $1 BILLION AND $3 BILLION	-	-
4	BETWEEN $500 MILLION AND $1 BILLION	-	-
5	BETWEEN $300 MILLION AND $500 MILLION	3 OR MORE	-
6	BETWEEN $300 MILLION AND $500 MILLION	2 OR FEWER	-
7	BETWEEN $100 MILLION AND $300 MILLION	3 OR MORE	METROPOLITAN AREA
8	BETWEEN $100 MILLION AND $300 MILLION	3 OR MORE	NON-METROPOLITAN AREA
9	BETWEEN $100 MILLION AND $300 MILLION	2 OR FEWER	METROPOLITAN AREA
10	BETWEEN $100 MILLION AND $300 MILLION	2 OR FEWER	NON-METROPOLITAN AREA
11	BETWEEN $50 MILLION AND $100 MILLION	3 OR MORE	METROPOLITAN AREA
12	BETWEEN $50 MILLION AND $100 MILLION	3 OR MORE	NON-METROPOLITAN AREA
13	BETWEEN $50 MILLION AND $100 MILLION	2 OR FEWER	METROPOLITAN AREA
14	BETWEEN $50 MILLION AND $100 MILLION	2 OR FEWER	NON-METROPOLITAN AREA
15	BETWEEN $25 MILLION AND $50 MILLION	2 OR MORE	METROPOLITAN AREA
16	BETWEEN $25 MILLION AND $50 MILLION	2 OR MORE	NON-METROPOLITAN AREA
17	BETWEEN $25 MILLION AND $50 MILLION	1	METROPOLITAN AREA
18	BETWEEN $25 MILLION AND $50 MILLION	1	NON-METROPOLITAN AREA
19	BETWEEN $10 MILLION AND $25 MILLION	2 OR MORE	METROPOLITAN AREA
20	BETWEEN $10 MILLION AND $25 MILLION	2 OR MORE	NON-METROPOLITAN AREA
21	BETWEEN $10 MILLION AND $25 MILLION	1	METROPOLITAN AREA
22	BETWEEN $10 MILLION AND $25 MILLION	1	NON-METROPOLITAN AREA
23	LESS THAN OR EQUAL TO $10 MILLION	-	METROPOLITAN AREA
24	LESS THAN OR EQUAL TO $10 MILLION	-	NON-METROPOLITAN AREA
25	WERE ESTABLISHED WITHIN THE LAST THREE YEARS, AND HAVE ASSETS LESS THAN OR EQUAL TO $25 MILLION		

*ASSET FIGURE USED IS LATEST QUARTERLY AVERAGE ASSETS (FROM THE FFIEC CALL REPORT SCHEDULE RC-K).
**METROPOLITAN STATUS IS DETERMINED BY LOCATION IN AN MSA (METROPOLITAN STATISTICAL AREA).

APPENDIX B - PEER GROUP REPORT

Page samples of the UBPR Peer Group Report follow. Items are grouped on these pages as they are grouped on various UBPR pages. For definitions of the items on these pages, refer to UBPR item definitions in Section III as follows:

Peer Group Page	UBPR Page
01	01
02	03
03	06
04	07
05	08
06	09 & 10
07	10 & 11
08	05

Date formats are the same as for comparable UBPR pages. See Appendix A for a definition of date formats.

FEDERAL FINANCIAL INSTITUTIONS EXAMINATION COUNCIL
UNIFORM BANK PERFORMANCE REPORT
PEER GROUP DATA
AS OF MM/DD/YY

INFORMATION

THE FOLLOWING PAGES CONTAIN A SUMMARY OF THE PEER GROUP DATA COMPILED AND USED IN THE UNIFORM BANK PERFORMANCE REPORT (UBPR). THE INFORMATION IS ASSEMBLED IN PEER GROUP ORDER AND ARRANGED IN SECTIONS WHICH CLOSELY CORRESPOND TO THE PRESENT UBPR FORMAT. DETAILED DESCRIPTIONS OF THE PEER GROUPS ARE PROVIDED IN THE APPENDIX SECTION OF THIS REPORT. MORE SPECIFIC INFORMATION CONCERNING THE RATIOS MAY BE FOUND IN "A USER'S GUIDE FOR THE UNIFORM BANK PERFORMANCE REPORT", A PUBLICATION OF THE FEDERAL FINANCIAL INSTITUTIONS EXAMINATION COUNCIL.

IF FEWER THAN FIVE BANKS' RATIO VALUES ARE AVAILABLE TO COMPUTE THE PEER GROUP FIGURES, A DOUBLE NUMBER SIGN (##) IS DISPLAYED.

NOTE:

THIS REPORT HAS BEEN PRODUCED FOR THE USE OF THE FEDERAL REGULATOR OF FINANCIAL INSTITUTIONS. ALL INFORMATION CONTAINED HEREIN WAS OBTAINED FROM SOURCES DEEMED RELIABLE; HOWEVER, NO GUARANTEE IS GIVEN AS TO THE ACCURACY OF THE DATA. USERS ARE CAUTIONED THAT ANY CONCLUSIONS DRAWN FROM THIS REPORT ARE THEIR OWN AND ARE NOT TO BE ATTRIBUTED TO THE FEDERAL BANK REGULATORS.

TABLE OF CONTENTS FOR EACH PEER GROUP

SECTIONS	PAGE NUMBER
SUMMARY RATIOS	01
INCOME INFORMATION:	
OVERHEAD, YIELD AND COST RATIOS	02
BALANCE SHEET INFORMATION:	
BALANCE SHEET - % COMPOSITION OF ASSETS & LIABILITIES	03
ANALYSIS OF LOAN & LEASE LOSS RESERVE AND LOAN MIX	04
ANALYSIS OF PAST DUE, NONACCRUAL AND RESTRUCTURED LOANS AND LEASES	05
MATURITY AND REPRICING DISTRIBUTION AND LIQUIDITY	06
INVESTMENT PORTFOLIO AND CAPITAL ANALYSIS	07
COMMITMENTS AND CONTINGENCIES	08
APPENDIX A - PEER GROUP DESCRIPTIONS	A1

APPENDIX B - PEER GROUP REPORT

UBPR PEER GROUP DATA   PAGE 01
PEER GROUP XX

SUMMARY RATIOS

	MM/DD/YY	MM/DD/YY	MM/DD/YY	MM/DD/YY	MM/DD/YY
NUMBER OF BANKS IN PEER GROUP	$999999999	$999999999	$999999999	$999999999	$999999999
EARNINGS AND PROFITABILITY					
PERCENT OF AVERAGE ASSETS:					
INTEREST INCOME (TE)	$999.99	$999.99	$999.99	$999.99	$999.99
- INTEREST EXPENSE	$999.99	$999.99	$999.99	$999.99	$999.99
NET INTEREST INCOME (TE)	$999.99	$999.99	$999.99	$999.99	$999.99
+ NON-INTEREST INCOME	$999.99	$999.99	$999.99	$999.99	$999.99
- OVERHEAD EXPENSE	$999.99	$999.99	$999.99	$999.99	$999.99
- PROVISION: LOAN&LEASE LOSSES	$999.99	$999.99	$999.99	$999.99	$999.99
= PRETAX OPERATING INCOME (TE)	$999.99	$999.99	$999.99	$999.99	$999.99
+ SECURITIES GAINS (LOSSES)	$999.99	$999.99	$999.99	$999.99	$999.99
= PRETAX NET OPERATING INC(TE)	$999.99	$999.99	$999.99	$999.99	$999.99
NET OPERATING INCOME	$999.99	$999.99	$999.99	$999.99	$999.99
ADJUSTED NET OPERATING INCOME	$999.99	$999.99	$999.99	$999.99	$999.99
ADJUSTED NET INCOME	$999.99	$999.99	$999.99	$999.99	$999.99
NET INCOME	$999.99	$999.99	$999.99	$999.99	$999.99
MARGIN ANALYSIS:					
AVG EARNING ASSETS TO AVG ASSTS	$999.99	$999.99	$999.99	$999.99	$999.99
AVG INT-BEARING FUNDS TO AV AST	$999.99	$999.99	$999.99	$999.99	$999.99
INT INC (TE) TO AVG EARN ASSETS	$999.99	$999.99	$999.99	$999.99	$999.99
INT EXPENSE TO AVG EARN ASSETS	$999.99	$999.99	$999.99	$999.99	$999.99
NET INT INC-TE TO AVG EARN ASST	$999.99	$999.99	$999.99	$999.99	$999.99
LOAN & LEASE ANALYSIS					
NET LOSS TO AVERAGE TOTAL LN&LS	$999.99	$999.99	$999.99	$999.99	$999.99
EARNINGS COVERAGE OF NET LOSS(X)	$999.99	$999.99	$999.99	$999.99	$999.99
LOSS RESERVE TO NET LOSSES (X)	$999.99	$999.99	$999.99	$999.99	$999.99
LOSS RESERVE TO TOTAL LN&LS	$999.99	$999.99	$999.99	$999.99	$999.99
% NON-CURRENT LOANS & LEASES	$999.99	$999.99	$999.99	$999.99	$999.99
LIQUIDITY					
VOLATILE LIABILITY DEPENDENCE	$999.99	$999.99	$999.99	$999.99	$999.99
NET LOANS & LEASES TO ASSETS	$999.99	$999.99	$999.99	$999.99	$999.99
CAPITALIZATION					
MEMBER PRIMARY CAP TO AVG ASSETS	$999.99	$999.99	$999.99	$999.99	$999.99
NONMEMBER PRIMARY CAP TO AVG AST	$999.99	$999.99	$999.99	$999.99	$999.99
CASH DIVIDENDS TO NET INCOME	$999.99	$999.99	$999.99	$999.99	$999.99
RETAIN EARNS TO AVG TOTAL EQUITY	$999.99	$999.99	$999.99	$999.99	$999.99
GROWTH RATES					
ASSETS	$999.99	$999.99	$999.99	$999.99	$999.99
MEMBER PRIMARY CAPITAL	$999.99	$999.99	$999.99	$999.99	$999.99
NONMEMBER PRIMARY CAPITAL	$999.99	$999.99	$999.99	$999.99	$999.99
NET LOANS & LEASES	$999.99	$999.99	$999.99	$999.99	$999.99
VOLATILE LIABILITIES	$999.99	$999.99	$999.99	$999.99	$999.99

APPENDIX B - PEER GROUP REPORT

if peer equals 7 or 8 or 9 or 10 then

UBPR PEER GROUP DATA
PEER GROUP XX

PAGE 02

OVERHEAD, YIELD AND COST RATIOS

PERCENT OF AVERAGE ASSETS	MM/DD/YY	MM/DD/YY	MM/DD/YY	MM/DD/YY	MM/DD/YY
PERSONNEL EXPENSE	$999.99	$999.99	$999.99	$999.99	$999.99
OCCUPANCY EXPENSE	$999.99	$999.99	$999.99	$999.99	$999.99
OTHER OPER EXP(INCL INTANGIBLES)	$999.99	$999.99	$999.99	$999.99	$999.99
TOTAL OVERHEAD EXPENSE	$999.99	$999.99	$999.99	$999.99	$999.99
:INCLUDING INT ON MORT & LEASES	$999.99	$999.99	$999.99	$999.99	$999.99
OVERHEAD LESS NON-INT INCOME	$999.99	$999.99	$999.99	$999.99	$999.99
OTHER INCOME & EXPENSE RATIOS:					
AVG PERSONNEL EXP PER EMPL($000)	$999.99	$999.99	$999.99	$999.99	$999.99
AVG ASSETS PER EMPL ($MILLION)	$999.99	$999.99	$999.99	$999.99	$999.99
MARGINAL TAX RATE	$999.99	$999.99	$999.99	$999.99	$999.99
YIELD ON OR COST OF:					
TOTAL LOANS & LEASES (TE)	$999.99	$999.99	$999.99	$999.99	$999.99
TOTAL LOANS	$999.99	$999.99	$999.99	$999.99	$999.99
REAL ESTATE**	$999.99	$999.99	$999.99	$999.99	$999.99
COMMERCIAL TIME, DEM, OTH**	$999.99	$999.99	$999.99	$999.99	$999.99
INSTALLMENT**	$999.99	$999.99	$999.99	$999.99	$999.99
CREDIT CARD PLANS**	$999.99	$999.99	$999.99	$999.99	$999.99
MEMO: AGRICULTURAL LNS IN ABOVE	$999.99	$999.99	$999.99	$999.99	$999.99
LOANS IN FOREIGN OFFICES	$999.99	$999.99	$999.99	$999.99	$999.99
TOTAL INVESTMENT SECURITIES (TE)	$999.99	$999.99	$999.99	$999.99	$999.99
U.S. TREASURIES & AGENCIES	$999.99	$999.99	$999.99	$999.99	$999.99
TAX-EXEMPT MUNICIPALS (BOOK)	$999.99	$999.99	$999.99	$999.99	$999.99
TAX-EXEMPT MUNICIPALS (TE)	$999.99	$999.99	$999.99	$999.99	$999.99
OTHER SECURITIES	$999.99	$999.99	$999.99	$999.99	$999.99
INTEREST-BEARING BANK BALANCES	$999.99	$999.99	$999.99	$999.99	$999.99
FEDERAL FUNDS SOLD & RESALES	$999.99	$999.99	$999.99	$999.99	$999.99
TOTAL INT-BEARING DEPOSITS	$999.99	$999.99	$999.99	$999.99	$999.99
TRANSACTION ACCOUNTS	$999.99	$999.99	$999.99	$999.99	$999.99
MONEY MARKET DEPOSIT ACCOUNTS	$999.99	$999.99	$999.99	$999.99	$999.99
OTHER SAVINGS DEPOSITS	$999.99	$999.99	$999.99	$999.99	$999.99
LARGE CERTIFICATES OF DEPOSIT	$999.99	$999.99	$999.99	$999.99	$999.99
ALL OTHER TIME DEPOSITS	$999.99	$999.99	$999.99	$999.99	$999.99
FOREIGN OFFICE DEPOSITS	$999.99	$999.99	$999.99	$999.99	$999.99
FEDERAL FUNDS PURCH & REPOS	$999.99	$999.99	$999.99	$999.99	$999.99
OTHER BORROWED MONEY	$999.99	$999.99	$999.99	$999.99	$999.99
SUBORDINATED NOTES & DEBENTURES	$999.99	$999.99	$999.99	$999.99	$999.99
ALL INTEREST-BEARING FUNDS	$999.99	$999.99	$999.99	$999.99	$999.99

**BANKS UNDER $300 MILLION IN TOTAL ASSETS REPORT THIS LOAN DETAIL (BY TYPE) USING THEIR OWN INTERNAL CATEGORIZATION SYSTEMS.

113

APPENDIX B - PEER GROUP REPORT

UBPR PEER GROUP DATA   PAGE 03
PEER GROUP XX

BALANCE SHEET - PERCENTAGE COMPOSITION OF ASSETS AND LIABILITIES

ASSETS, PERCENT OF AVG ASSETS	MM/DD/YY	MM/DD/YY	MM/DD/YY	MM/DD/YY	MM/DD/YY
TOTAL LOANS	$999.99	$999.99	$999.99	$999.99	$999.99
LEASE FINANCING RECEIVABLES	$999.99	$999.99	$999.99	$999.99	$999.99
LESS: RESERVES	$999.99	$999.99	$999.99	$999.99	$999.99
NET LOANS & LEASES	$999.99	$999.99	$999.99	$999.99	$999.99
SECURITIES OVER 1 YEAR	$999.99	$999.99	$999.99	$999.99	$999.99
SUBTOTAL	$999.99	$999.99	$999.99	$999.99	$999.99
INTEREST-BEARING BANK BALANCES	$999.99	$999.99	$999.99	$999.99	$999.99
FEDERAL FUNDS SOLD & RESALES	$999.99	$999.99	$999.99	$999.99	$999.99
TRADING ACCOUNT ASSETS	$999.99	$999.99	$999.99	$999.99	$999.99
DEBT SECURITIES 1 YEAR & LESS	$999.99	$999.99	$999.99	$999.99	$999.99
TEMPORARY INVESTMENTS	$999.99	$999.99	$999.99	$999.99	$999.99
TOTAL EARNING ASSETS	$999.99	$999.99	$999.99	$999.99	$999.99
NON-INT CASH & DUE FROM BANKS	$999.99	$999.99	$999.99	$999.99	$999.99
PREMISES, FIX ASSTS & CAP LEASES	$999.99	$999.99	$999.99	$999.99	$999.99
OTHER REAL ESTATE OWNED	$999.99	$999.99	$999.99	$999.99	$999.99
ACCEPTANCES & OTHER ASSETS	$999.99	$999.99	$999.99	$999.99	$999.99
SUBTOTAL	$999.99	$999.99	$999.99	$999.99	$999.99
TOTAL ASSETS	$999.99	$999.99	$999.99	$999.99	$999.99
STANDBY LETTERS OF CREDIT	$999.99	$999.99	$999.99	$999.99	$999.99
LIABILITIES, PERCENT OF AVG ASST					
DEMAND DEPOSITS	$999.99	$999.99	$999.99	$999.99	$999.99
ALL NOW & ATS ACCOUNTS	$999.99	$999.99	$999.99	$999.99	$999.99
MMDA SAVINGS	$999.99	$999.99	$999.99	$999.99	$999.99
OTHER SAVINGS DEPOSITS	$999.99	$999.99	$999.99	$999.99	$999.99
TIME DEPOSITS UNDER $100M	$999.99	$999.99	$999.99	$999.99	$999.99
CORE DEPOSITS	$999.99	$999.99	$999.99	$999.99	$999.99
TIME DEPOSITS OVER $100M	$999.99	$999.99	$999.99	$999.99	$999.99
DEPOSITS IN FOREIGN OFFICES	$999.99	$999.99	$999.99	$999.99	$999.99
FEDERAL FUNDS PURCH & REPOS	$999.99	$999.99	$999.99	$999.99	$999.99
OTHER BORROWINGS (+NOTE OPT)	$999.99	$999.99	$999.99	$999.99	$999.99
VOLATILE LIABILITIES	$999.99	$999.99	$999.99	$999.99	$999.99
ACCEPTANCES & OTHER LIABILITIES	$999.99	$999.99	$999.99	$999.99	$999.99
TOTAL LIABILITIES (INCL MORTG)	$999.99	$999.99	$999.99	$999.99	$999.99
SUBORDINATED NOTES& DEBENTURES	$999.99	$999.99	$999.99	$999.99	$999.99
ALL COMMON & PREFERRED CAPITAL	$999.99	$999.99	$999.99	$999.99	$999.99
TOTAL LIABILITIES & CAPITAL	$999.99	$999.99	$999.99	$999.99	$999.99
TOTAL BROKERED DEPOSITS	$999.99	$999.99	$999.99	$999.99	$999.99

APPENDIX B - PEER GROUP REPORT

if peer less than 7 then

UBPR PEER GROUP DATA
PEER GROUP XX

PAGE 05

ANALYSIS OF PAST DUE, NONACCRUAL AND RESTRUCTURED LOANS AND LEASES

% OF NON-CURRENT LN&LS BY TYPE	MM/DD/YY	MM/DD/YY	MM/DD/YY	MM/DD/YY	MM/DD/YY
REAL ESTATE LNS-90+ DAYS P/D	$999.99	$999.99	$999.99	$999.99	$999.99
-NONACCRUAL	$999.99	$999.99	$999.99	$999.99	$999.99
-TOTAL	$999.99	$999.99	$999.99	$999.99	$999.99
COML & INDUST LNS-90+ DAYS P/D	$999.99	$999.99	$999.99	$999.99	$999.99
-NONACCRUAL	$999.99	$999.99	$999.99	$999.99	$999.99
-TOTAL	$999.99	$999.99	$999.99	$999.99	$999.99
LOANS TO INDIVDLS-90+ DAYS P/D	$999.99	$999.99	$999.99	$999.99	$999.99
-NONACCRUAL	$999.99	$999.99	$999.99	$999.99	$999.99
-TOTAL	$999.99	$999.99	$999.99	$999.99	$999.99
AGRICULTURAL LNS-90+ DAYS P/D	$999.99	$999.99	$999.99	$999.99	$999.99
-NONACCRUAL	$999.99	$999.99	$999.99	$999.94	$999.99
-TOTAL	$999.99	$999.99	$999.99	$999.99	$999.99
OTHER LN&LS-90+ DAYS P/D	$999.99	$999.99	$999.99	$999.99	$999.99
-NONACCRUAL	$999.99	$999.99	$999.99	$999.99	$999.99
-TOTAL	$999.99	$999.99	$999.99	$999.99	$999.99
FOREIGN OFF LN&LS-90+ DAYS P/D	$999.99	$999.99	$999.99	$999.99	$999.99
-NONACCRUAL	$999.99	$999.99	$999.99	$999.99	$999.99
-TOTAL	$999.99	$999.99	$999.99	$999.99	$999.99
TOTAL LN&LS-90+ DAYS P/D	$999.99	$999.99	$999.99	$999.99	$999.99
-NONACCRUAL	$999.99	$999.99	$999.99	$999.99	$999.99
-TOTAL	$999.99	$999.99	$999.99	$999.99	$999.99
OTHER PERTINENT RATIOS:					
NON-CURRENT LN&LS TO TOTAL ASSTS	$999.99	$999.99	$999.99	$999.99	$999.99
IENC-LOANS TO TOTAL LOANS	$999.99	$999.99	$999.99	$999.99	$999.99
% CURRENT RESTRUCT DEBT BY TYPE:					
LOANS SECURED BY REAL ESTATE	$999.99	$999.99	$999.99	$999.99	$999.99
COMMERCIAL AND INDUSTRIAL LNS	$999.99	$999.99	$999.99	$999.99	$999.99
AGRICULTURAL LOANS	$999.99	$999.99	$999.99	$999.99	$999.99
ALL OTHER LOANS & LEASES	$999.99	$999.99	$999.99	$999.99	$999.99
FOREIGN OFFICE LOANS & LEASES	$999.99	$999.99	$999.99	$999.99	$999.99

115

APPENDIX B - PEER GROUP REPORT

UBPR PEER GROUP DATA
PEER GROUP XX

MATURITY AND REPRICING DISTRIBUTION AND LIQUIDITY

MATURITY AND REPRICING DISTRIBUTION AS OF MM/DD/YY

CUMULATIVE PERCENT OF ITEM

ASSETS	ITEM TOTAL AS A PERCENT OF ASSETS	PERCENT REPRICED WITHIN 3 MONTHS	PERCENT REPRICED WITHIN 12 MONTHS	PERCENT REPRICED WITHIN 5 YEARS
LOANS AND LEASES (EXCL NONACC)	$999.99	$999.99	$999.99	$999.99
FIXED RATE BY MATURITY	$999.99	$999.99	$999.99	$999.99
FLOATING RATE BY REP INTERVAL	$999.99	$999.99	$999.99	$999.99
DEBT SECURITIES	$999.99	$999.99	$999.99	$999.99
FIXED RATE BY MATURITY	$999.99	$999.99	$999.99	$999.99
FLOATING RATE BY REP INTERVAL	$999.99	$999.99	$999.99	$999.99
FEDERAL FUNDS SOLD (OVERNIGHT)	$999.99	100.00		
SECURITIES PURCHASED UNDER AGREEMENT TO RESELL*	$999.99			
INTEREST-BEARING BANK BALANCES*	$999.99			
TRADING ACCOUNT ASSETS	$999.99	100.00		
TOTAL INTEREST-BEARING ASSETS	$999.99			
LIABILITIES				
DEPOSITS IN FOREIGN OFFICES*	$999.99			
CD'S OF $100,000 OR MORE	$999.99	$999.99	$999.99	$999.99
FIXED RATE BY MATURITY	$999.99	$999.99	$999.99	$999.99
FLOATING RATE BY REP INTERVAL	$999.99	$999.99	$999.99	$999.99
OTHER TIME DEPOSITS*	$999.99	$999.99		
MONEY MARKET DEPOSIT ACCOUNTS	$999.99	100.00		
OTHER SAVINGS DEP (EXCL MMDA)*	$999.99			
NOW ACCOUNTS	$999.99	100.00		
FEDERAL FUNDS PURCH (OVERNIGHT)	$999.99	100.00		
SECURITIES SOLD UNDER AGREEMENT TO REPURCHASE*	$999.99			
OTHER BORROWED MONEY*	$999.99			
SUB NOTES & DEBENTURES*	$999.99			
TREASURY NOTES	$999.99	100.00		
TOTAL INTEREST-BEARING LIABS	$999.99			

LIQUIDITY RATIOS	MM/DD/YY	MM/DD/YY	MM/DD/YY	MM/DD/YY	MM/DD/YY
VOLATILE LIABILITY DEPENDENCE	$999.99	$999.99	$999.99	$999.99	$999.99
TEMP INV TO VOLATILE LIABILITIES	$999.99	$999.99	$999.99	$999.99	$999.99
BROKER DEPOSITS TO DEPOSITS	$999.99	$999.99	$999.99	$999.99	$999.99
TEMP INV LESS VOL LIAB TO ASSETS	$999.99	$999.99	$999.99	$999.99	$999.99
NET LOANS & LEASES TO DEPOSITS	$999.99	$999.99	$999.99	$999.99	$999.99
NET LN&LS TO CORE DEPOSITS	$999.99	$999.99	$999.99	$999.99	$999.99
NET LOANS & LEASES TO ASSETS	$999.99	$999.99	$999.99	$999.99	$999.99
NET LN&LS & SBLC TO ASSETS	$999.99	$999.99	$999.99	$999.99	$999.99
TEMP INVESTMENTS TO ASSETS	$999.99	$999.99	$999.99	$999.99	$999.99
CORE DEPOSITS TO ASSETS	$999.99	$999.99	$999.99	$999.99	$999.99
VOLATILE LIABILITIES TO ASSETS	$999.99	$999.99	$999.99	$999.99	$999.99

*INDICATED ITEMS ARE NOT REPORTED BY MATURITY/REPRICING INTERVAL AS OF MARCH 31, 1988.
OTHER TIME DEPOSITS ARE NOT BROKEN DOWN BEYOND THREE MONTHS.

5

Analysis of Bank Financial Statements

Having reviewed financial statements in Chapter 3 and the analytical tools used to evaluate financial statement data in Chapter 4, the next step is to perform the analysis. Two banks are analyzed here–one a small rural bank, Farmers' State, the other a large urban bank, City National–over a five year period using the financial statements and other information contained in the Uniform Bank Performance Report.

Although the names and time periods have been disguised, material used in this chapter is based on two real banks with the actual numbers drawn from the Report. The approach taken in this text is that the analyst can complete a performance evaluation of any insured commercial banking institution in the U.S. using the financial statements and analytical tools from the Uniform Bank Performance Report, described in Chapters 3 and 4, regardless of the type of bank or whether its stock is publicly traded. A comparable analysis could also be developed from published financial statements using the basic financial statements discussed in Chapter 3 and the analytical tools described in Chapter 4. The advantage of the Uniform Bank Performance Report is that it presents standardized information on a timely basis and is available both to banks and the general public. (See order information in Chapter 3.)

Size of bank. Before beginning the analysis, it is useful to look at some general characteristics of large versus small banks. Because banks vary considerably in size, location, and many other factors, the analysis will include peer group comparisons for each institution. In general, large banks tend to be oriented more towards business customers–which is reflected both in the loan portfolio and the funding sources, such as a heavier reliance on large, negotiable certificates of deposit. In terms of balance sheet structure, large banks have relatively less equity capital, a larger proportion of loans, and fewer security holdings than small banks. Because large banks do not carry as much liquidity, they typically use more sophisticated liability management–fed funds borrowing, for example–to meet liquidity needs. It is interesting to see how closely the two banks discussed in this chapter conform to the general characteristics of small versus large banks.

Relationship between balance sheet and income statement. In analyzing any firm, it is important to keep in mind the relationship between the balance sheet and the income statement. The balance sheet is a stock statement, showing assets, liabilities, and capital at a point in time, thus the accounts may fluctuate considerably from one day to the next. The income statement presents the flow of funds–revenues and expenses–over an accounting period. The statements are integrally related to each other and must be reviewed in tandem.

For example, the provision for loan losses affects net income for the period, the net loan asset account on the balance sheet, as well as the reserve for loan losses that is included in calculating primary capital. It is also important to recognize that financial ratios based on financial statement numbers are presented in percentage form, and the analyst should use these ratios in conjunction with the actual dollar amounts shown in the financial statements to avoid misinterpretations.

Risk vs. Return. In evaluating bank performance, the analyst simultaneously monitors the relationship between risk and return. Risk can magnify a firm's profitability through financial leverage, but risk also carries a cost, the potential for loss–and even bank failure–from inadequate or improper risk management.

Factors that cannot be qualified. The analyst should be aware that in spite of the thirty financial ratios that will be used to analyze profitability and risk and the hundreds of ratios and other financial measures that can be used for the same purpose, there are many important aspects of financial statement analysis that cannot be quantified. These intangibles include: employee relations with management, morale and efficiency of employees, the firm's reputation with its customers, the bank's prestige in the community, the quality of management, and provisions for continuity of management. Such factors are of considerable importance in evaluating a bank, but information about these aspects is available only indirectly–through how well the bank performs–in the financial statements.

Missing information. Some information that is relevant to bank analysis is not available in the Uniform Bank Performance Report in its current format. The interest rate "gap" discussed in Chapter 4 in relation to interest rate risk can only be approximated from the data reported. The Report does not show the number of branches for those banking institutions that are engaged in branch banking, but this information is available in the *Rand McNally International Banking Directory* and *Moody's Bank and Finance Manual*. The balance sheet format in the Uniform Bank Performance Report shows only "all common and preferred capital," with no breakdown of specific capital accounts. Nor does the additional data in the Report on "Capital Analysis" contain any information on the specific accounts comprising "common equity," such as common stock, paid-in capital or surplus, and retained earnings. It is therefore impossible for the analyst to trace and explain changes in the equity accounts.

Quality of reporting. It should also be noted that in spite of the uniformity of bank reporting required by bank regulatory authorities and the availability of this information in the Uniform Bank Performance Report, the quality of financial statement data varies from bank to bank and from one reporting period to the next. The result is that the "bottom line" figure for net income may not be fully representative of the firm's future earnings potential. Financial statements are prepared according to the "accrual" rather than the "cash" basis of accounting. This means that income and expenses are allocated to accounting periods, regardless of when the cash is actually collected or paid out. For example, banks are permitted to "accrue" interest on loans for up to ninety days before a loan goes on nonaccrual status. The annual provision for loan losses requires an estimation by management of the probable charge-offs for loans reported on the balance sheet that will be uncollectable.

Further, banks may execute financial transactions that are nonrecurring and/or nonoperating in nature. If the analyst is seeking an earnings figure that reflects the ability of the bank to generate income in the future, such transactions–that are not part of ongoing business–should be reviewed and possibly eliminated from earnings. One such transaction would be the gain (or loss) from the sale of property. Banks sometimes sell an asset in order to generate cash and/or profits during lean periods. In 1985 Bank America Corporation sold its headquarters complex for a huge profit in order to boost earnings. Obviously such a deal is both nonrecurring and nonoperating and should be ignored in measuring the firm's ability to generate future profits. Gains (and losses) from sales of securities should also be examined for the impact on earnings since they are nonoperating sources of income made largely at the discretion of management with respect to magnitude and timing.

Farmers' State Bank

Tables 5-1, 5-2, and 5-3 show the financial statements and key analytical measures for Farmers' State bank–classified in a peer group with insured commercial banks having assets between $100 million and $300 million with two or less banking offices, located in a non-metropolitan area–for the 19X5–19X9 period. (Percentile rankings have not been provided with the peer group averages for reasons of readability, but these figures are available in the Uniform Bank Performance Report and were included with the ratios in Chapter 4.)

Profitability. Farmers' State consistently generated a profit during the 19X5-19X9 period, although the amount of profit has never matched the peak year of 19X5. Farmers' State significantly outperformed its peer group, as measured by the ratio of net income/average assets, in 19X9, 19X8, and 19X5. The worst year in this five year period was 19X6, both in terms of the absolute amount of profit and in relation to the peer group.

Net interest income is the major source of income at Farmers' State while noninterest income is insignificant and consistently lower than its peer group. Farmers' State has kept overhead expenses under control. The provision for loan losses has risen markedly since 19X5 to a high of $3.2

Table 5-1
FARMERS' STATE BANK
BALANCE SHEET
Assets, Liabilities, and Capital ($000) at December 31,

Assets:		19x9	19X8	19X7	19X6	19X5
(1)	Real Estate Loans	50393	38975	36539	31232	31710
(2)	Commercial Loans	9615	11381	12956	15247	20218
(3)	Individual Loans	8824	10640	15970	15299	12814
(4)	Agricultural Loans	20680	19654	20602	23066	21848
(5)	Other LN & LS–Domestic	3684	4025	3134	3976	4791
(6)	LN & LS–Foreign	0	0	0	0	0
(7)	Gross Loans & Leases	93196	84675	89201	88820	91381
(8)	Less: Unearned Income	89	282	736	949	913
(9)	Reserves	3006	2536	1247	679	440
(10)	Net Loans & Leases	90101	81857	87218	87192	90028
(11)	U.S. Treas & Agen Securities	54082	44848	31556	39213	34007
(12)	Municipal Securities	32789	34616	41632	27123	29817
(13)	Foreign Debt Securities	0	0	0	0	0
(14)	All Other Securities	0	0	25	25	0
(15)	Int-Bearing Bank Bal.	0	1000	0	0	3850
(16)	Fed Funds Sold & Resales	10500	1500	0	2500	10200
(17)	Trading Account Assets	0	0	0	0	0
(18)	Total Investments	97371	81964	73213	68861	77874
(19)	Total Earning Assets	187472	163821	160431	156053	167902
(20)	Non-Int Cash, Due Fr Banks	9039	10522	8924	10078	6412
(21)	Acceptances	0	0	0	0	0
(22)	Prem, Fx Assets, Cap Leases	2229	2398	2489	2633	2714
(23)	Other Real Estate Owned	2282	3012	3102	2762	30
(24)	Inv. Uncon. Subsidiaries	0	0	0	0	0
(25)	Other Assets	4951	4014	3866	3986	4188
(26)	Total Assets	205973	183767	178812	175512	181246
(27)	Avg. Assets During Qtr.	200462	180049	171811	173445	177615
Liabilities & Capital:						
(28)	Demand Deposits	23063	22528	25322	23555	23954
(29)	All NOW & ATS Accounts	6021	5322	4659	4262	3453
(30)	MMDA Accounts	41402	49797	31323	26575	32175
(31)	Other Savings Deposits	3097	2992	3287	3956	3751
(32)	Nonbrok. Time Deps <$100M	31707	28954	26704	27508	43710
(33)	Core Deposits	105290	109593	91295	85856	107043
(34)	All Brokered Deposits	0	0	0	0	0
(35)	Nonbrok. Time Deps >$100M	83009	57665	70373	72830	57745
(36)	Deps in Foreign Offices	0	0	0	0	0
(37)	Total Deposits	188299	167258	161668	158686	164788
(38)	Fed Funds Purch & Resale	0	0	800	0	0
(39)	Other Borrowings	0	0	0	0	0
(40)	Volatile Liabilities	83009	57665	71173	72830	57745
(41)	Accept.& Other Liabilities	3546	3101	3627	3996	3517
(42)	Total Liab. (Incl. Mtg)	191845	170359	166095	162682	168305
(43)	Sub.Notes & Deben.	0	0	0	0	0
(44)	All Common & Pfd Capital	14128	13408	12717	12830	12941
(45)	Total Liab. & Capital	205973	183767	178812	175512	181246
Memoranda:						
(46)	Officer, Shholder Ln(#)	3	2	4	4	7
(47)	Officer, Shholder Ln ($)	276	176	387	309	1286
(48)	Direct, Indirect Invest in RE	0	0	0	0	0
(49)	Total Curr. Restruc. Debt	0	0	0	0	0

Table 5-2
FARMERS' STATE BANK
INCOME STATEMENT
REVENUE AND EXPENSES ($000)
For Period ending December 31,

		19x9	19X8	19X7	19X6	19X5
(1)	Interest & Fees on loans	8931	9192	10251	11323	9647
(2)	Income from lease finc.	0	0	0	0	0
(3)	Fully taxable	8880	9142	10180	11206	NA
(4)	Tax Exempt	51	50	71	117	NA
(5)	Estimated tax benefit	38	21	43	0	NA
(6)	Income on loans & leases (TE)	8969	9213	10294	11323	NA
(7)	U.S.Treas, agency securities	3735	3025	4337	4122	2998
(8)	Tax exempt security income	3097	3571	2058	2277	2964
(9)	Estimated tax benefit	1882	2103	1390	1129	2442
(10)	Other securities income	13	0	1	0	0
(11)	Invest. interest income (TE)	8727	8699	7786	7528	8404
(12)	Int. Fed funds sold,resales	192	83	244	365	407
(13)	Int on due from banks	27	5	0	54	738
(14)	Trading account income	0	0	0	0	0
(15)	Total interest income (TE)	17915	18001	18324	19270	19196
(16)	Interest on foreign deposits	0	0	0	0	0
(17)	Interest on CDs over $100M	3248	2924	3919	4825	4268
(18)	Interest on other deposits	6757	7167	7138	8621	7781
(19)	Int of Fed funds purch/repos	16	59	24	83	0
(20)	Interest borrowed money	0	50	11	18	0
(21)	Int on mortgages & leases	0	0	0	0	0
(22)	Int on sub notes & debentures	0	0	0	0	0
(23)	Total interest expense	10021	10200	11092	13547	12254
(24)	Net interest income (TE)	7894	7801	7232	5723	6942
(25)	Non-interest income	571	577	569	491	483
(26)	Adjusted operating income (TE)	8465	8378	7801	6214	7425
(27)	Overhead expense	3624	3876	3435	2823	2851
(28)	Provision loan/lease loss	1294	3208	1980	1142	241
(29)	Prov. allocated transfer risk	NA	NA	NA	NA	NA
(30)	Pretax operating income (TE)	3547	1294	2386	2249	4333
(31)	Securities gains (losses)	1240	3331	734	209	732
(32)	Pretax net operating inc (TE)	4787	4625	3120	2458	5065
(33)	Applicable income taxes	347	8	0	0	-125
(34)	Current tax equiv adjustments	1920	2125	1433	1129	2442
(35)	Other tax equiv adjustments	0	0	0	0	0
(36)	Applicable income tax (TE)	2267	2133	1433	1129	2317
(37)	Net operating income	2520	2492	1687	1329	2748
(38)	Net extraordinary items	0	0	0	0	0
(39)	Net income	2520	2492	1687	1329	2748
(40)	Cash dividends declared	1800	1800	1800	1440	1800
(41)	Retained earnings	720	692	-113	-111	948
(42)	Memo: net int'l income	0	0	0	0	0

Table 5-3
Farmers' State Bank

Financial Ratio (percent)	19X9 FSB	19X9 Peer	19X8 FSB	19X8 Peer	19X7 FSB	19X7 Peer	19X6 FSB	19X6 Peer	19X5 FSB	19X5 Peer
Profitability:										
(1) Net income/average assets	1.31	0.84	1.41	0.68	1.00	1.03	0.77	1.04	1.60	1.12
(2) Net interest income/average assets	4.10	3.90	4.41	4.15	4.28	4.43	3.31	4.34	4.05	4.54
(3) Non-interest income/average assets	0.30	0.58	0.33	0.64	0.34	0.64	0.28	0.60	0.28	0.55
(4) Overhead expense/average assets	1.88	2.56	2.19	2.66	2.03	2.60	1.63	2.51	1.66	2.47
(5) Provision for loan and lease losses/average assets	0.67	0.68	1.81	1.01	1.17	0.73	0.66	0.54	0.14	0.53
(6) Net securities gains or losses/average assets	0.64	0.02	1.88	0.11	0.43	0.04	0.12	0.01	0.43	0.00
(7) Net extraordinary items/average assets	0.00	0.01	0.00	0.01	0.00	0.00	0.00	-0.01	0.00	0.00
(8) Applicable income taxes/average assets	1.18	0.64	1.21	0.70	0.85	0.83	0.65	0.87	1.35	0.92
(9) Interest income/average assets	9.31	8.88	10.18	9.71	10.85	10.80	11.16	11.54	11.21	11.19
(10) Interest expense/average assets	5.21	4.99	5.77	5.57	6.57	6.39	7.85	7.26	7.16	6.64
(11) Interest income/average earning assets	10.01	9.56	11.44	10.49	12.28	11.72	12.56	12.55	12.00	12.21
(12) Interest expense/average earning assets	5.60	5.38	6.48	6.03	7.43	6.92	8.83	7.88	7.66	7.25
(13) Personnel expense/average assets	0.96	1.22	1.02	1.29	1.08	1.32	0.94	1.30	0.92	1.27
(14) Occupancy expense/average assets	0.18	0.33	0.20	0.35	0.21	0.35	0.22	0.35	0.28	0.37
(15) Other operating expense/average assets	0.74	0.95	0.98	0.97	0.75	0.92	0.47	0.86	0.47	0.83
Capital Risk:										
(16) Primary capital/adjusted average assets	8.42	8.85	8.73	8.82	8.07	8.74	7.76	8.60	7.52	8.54
(17) Growth rate: assets	12.08	3.51	2.77	4.01	1.88	5.43	-3.16	6.68	6.26	8.67
(18) Growth rate: primary capital	7.46	5.98	14.18	5.28	3.37	7.27	0.96	7.71	7.25	9.21
(19) Cash dividends/net operating income	71.43	45.75	72.23	47.30	106.70	45.03	108.35	46.83	65.50	40.19
Credit risk:										
(20) Net loss/total loans and leases	0.92	1.17	2.33	1.73	1.73	1.39	1.17	0.85	0.34	0.87
(21) Earnings coverage of net loss (X)	3.54	6.20	1.24	3.87	2.08	4.93	2.38	9.08	7.51	9.59
(22) Loss reserve/net loss (X)	3.65	2.99	1.32	1.50	0.88	1.71	0.71	3.03	1.55	2.87
(23) Loss reserve/total loans and leases	3.23	1.85	3.00	1.67	1.41	1.39	0.77	1.26	0.49	1.10
(24) Percent noncurrent loans and leases	2.44	3.02	2.56	3.11	1.83	2.86	3.08	2.47	2.06	1.99
(5) Provision loan loss/average assets	0.67	0.68	1.81	1.01	1.17	0.73	0.66	0.54	0.14	0.53
Liquidity:										
(25) Temporary investments/volatile liabilities	15.25	143.50	4.51	149.44	2.47	126.12	31.96	120.96	32.72	114.86
(26) Volatile liability dependence	40.24	-5.41	34.15	-7.93	43.75	-1.05	37.32	0.22	26.07	1.20
(27) Loans and leases/assets	43.74	48.70	44.54	48.95	48.78	52.16	49.68	52.83	49.67	50.86
Interest rate:										
(28) Gap	-18.25	-6.25								
Fraud risk:										
(29) Officer, shareholder loans/assets	0.13	0.18	0.10	0.22	0.22	0.20	0.15	N A	0.71	N A
Summary										
(30) Net income/average equity	16.74	9.98	17.34	8.69	12.44	13.05	9.77	13.30	21.06	13.98

million in 19X8, and the loan loss reserve (balance sheet) increased from $440 thousand in 19X5 to over $3 million in 19X9. Farmers' State has generated gains from securities transactions and has outperformed its peer group in security transactions in all five years. This income, however, has fluctuated from a high of $3.3 million in 19X8 to a low of $200 thousand in 19X6 and is neither a stable nor predictable source of income.

Total interest income for Farmers' State is divided almost equally between income on loans and income from investments. Investment interest income has been fairly stable over the period, while income on loans has decreased. It should be noted that the 19X5-19X9 was a period of declining interest rates in the economy. The rise in investment income is largely the result of increases in U.S. Treasury and Agency investments which are typically pledged against government deposits. Net loans at Farmers' State are about the same in 19X9 and 19X5, but the composition of the loan portfolio has shifted significantly towards real estate loans with declines in commercial and individual loans. Since real estate loans are generally perceived as posing a somewhat greater risk, this shift in composition may impact credit risk.

Although Farmers' State has had higher interest expense than its peers, as measured by interest expense/average assets and interest expense/average earning assets, the bank has generated relatively greater amounts of net interest income since 19X7 which means that it is earning more on its interest earnings assets.

There are several possible reasons that the analyst might want to explore by using supplemental data from the Uniform Bank Performance Report. The bank could have more loans, and loans typically generate more income. This is not the case, however, for Farmers' State; the bank's net loans/

assets (ratio twenty-seven) have been consistently lower than its peer group. Farmers' State must, then, be earning higher rates of interest on its earning assets. The Uniform Bank Performance Report shows the yield or cost of interest-earning/bearing assets and liabilities (on page three of the report).

Figure 5-1
Yields on Total Loans and Leases, Investment Securities

		Total Loans and Leases	Investment Securities
19X9	FSB	10.00	10.16
	Peer Group	10.45	9.21
19X8	FSB	11.18	11.83
	Peer Group	11.22	10.46
19X7	FSB	12.63	12.02
	Peer Group	12.35	11.40
19X6	FSB	13.88	11.18
	Peer Group	13.19	11.77
19X5	FSB	11.58	12.99
	Peer Group	12.80	12.01

Figure 5-1 shows the yields on total loans and leases and investment securities for Farmers' State and its peer group over the five-year period. This supplemental information reveals that Farmers' State's competitive edge is more the result of income on investments than from loans. Farmers' State actually earned less on total loans and leases than its peer group in 19X9, 19X8, and 19X5. The issue for the future is whether or not the bank can maintain its margins. Farmers' State's balance sheet reveals a steadily increasing proportion of U.S. Treasury and Agency securities and, within the loan portfolio, an increase in real estate loans. Yields earned on real estate loans and U.S. government securities for Farmers' State and its peer group are shown in Figure 5-2. It is apparent that Farmers' State is earning less than its peer group on both of the assets that have shown substantial increases in volume.

Figure 5-2
Yields on Real Estate Loans and U.S. Government Securities

19X9 Yields on:	Real Estate Loans	U.S. Treas. & Agency Sec.
Farmers' State	9.02	7.08
Peer Group	10.48	8.07

The higher interest earnings at Farmers' State stem in part from its management of rate sensitive assets and liabilities. During a period of falling interest rates, which has been the case for the 19X5-19X9 period, a bank benefits from holding more rate sensitive liabilities than assets–a negative gap. Farmers' State had a negative gap and one that was greater than its peer group in 19X9. If interest rates increase, Farmers' State's profits will be impaired by the negative gap. It appears that Farmers' State could have problems maintaining its competitive interest edge, particularly if interest rates rise.

Capital risk. Farmers' State has experienced erratic growth in assets during the 19X5-19X9 period with a more stable increase in primary capital. The ratio of primary capital to average assets is not out of line with the peer group. The dangers here in terms of capital risk are from the composition of asset growth and the extremely high dividend payout for Farmers' State. Much of the gain in assets is due to growth in real estate loans, the type of loan that typically produces considerable interest rate risk. Further, Farmers' State has paid out a far greater proportion of income to shareholders than its peers, thus inhibiting internal capital growth. In 19X7 and 19X6 Farmers' State paid out dividends greater than earnings. The income statement for Farmers' State reveals that the bank has maintained a constant cash dividend payment of $1.8 million per year with the exception of 19X6 when the payout was trimmed to $1.4 million as a result of low profits. Still, the dividend payment in 19X6 was more than the $1.3 million in earnings.

Many firms, both bank and nonbank, are reluctant to reduce dividend payments because of management fear that investors will read this as a signal of problems. The result is a constant or growing dividend payout regardless of the size of earnings or the amount of cash generated in a given year. Another factor in the case of Farmers' State's dividend policy could be the size of the institution and the type of ownership. A small organization may be fairly concentrated in the hands of one or very few owners who prefer profits to be paid out in cash rather than reinvested in the business. Because of the high dividend payout at Farmers' State–ranging from sixty-six percent to 108 percent of earnings–most of the bank's capital growth has resulted from contributions to the loan loss reserve.

Credit risk. Since 19X9 Farmers' State has had a higher loss reserve to total loans and leases than its peers and one that has been steadily rising. 19X5 was the best year of the period for Farmers' State from the standpoint of profitability, and part of the reason may have been an underallowance for loan losses that the bank had to make up in ensuing periods. The bank's net loss/total loans and leases, after steadily increasing between 19X5 and 19X8, was much lower in 19X9. This means that actual losses less recoveries relative to the total loan portfolio showed significant improvement in 19X9, also reflected in the provision for loan and lease losses to average assets which dropped considerably in 19X9 and the earnings coverage of net loss that improved to a level greater than the peer group for the first time. Farmers' State's percentage of noncurrent loans, after steadily increasing between 19X5 and 19X8, also dropped in 19X9.

There has been a substantial shift in Farmers' State's loan portfolio over the five year period with an increase of real estate loans and comparable reductions in commercial and individual loans. The shift in the loan composition may reflect a change in loan demand. Small banks in particular find that their loan composition is not fully under management's control. It could be that for Farmers' State this shift reflects a lessening of interest rate risk, as measured by the improvement in net loan losses. This would not usually be the case for real estate loans, however, and it may be that the bank is back in the same situation it was in 19X5, under-allowing for a riskier type of loan–in this case, real estate loans. The big jump in this category occurred primarily between 19X8 and 19X9. If Farmers' State is not adequately allowing for potential losses, the bank can expect a negative impact on profits in subsequent years and a deterioration in the ratios that measure interest rate risk. Figure 5-3 is taken from the Uniform Bank Performance Report and shows the percent of noncurrent loans and leases by type:

Figure 5-3
Percent of Noncurrent Loans and Leases, 19X9

	Farmers' State	Peer Group
Real Estate	3.87	2.87
Commercial	0.72	3.36
Installment	2.43	1.06
Total	2.44	3.00

These data reveal that Farmer's State had a higher percentage of noncurrent real estate loans in 19X9 than other types of loans and that this category for Farmers' State is higher than the peer group, suggesting that Farmers' State may be currently underallowing for loan losses.

Liquidity. Unlike most small banks, Farmers' State relies heavily on volatile liabilities–specifically jumbo CD's–as a funding source. Farmers' State has a volatile liability dependence ratio that is extremely high relative to the peer group's (which was actually negative during the three most recent years) and a temporary investments to volatile liabilities ratio much lower than the peer group. This signals potential liquidity problems should funding dry up. There is no way to determine from the financial statements why Farmers' State's relies so heavily on jumbo CD's or the degree to which this money might be unstable for the bank. Where small town banks are concerned, the owner can have a significant impact on such matters. For example, a large proportion of the CD's could be a wealthy owner's personal investment, meaning that the funds would actually be quite stable. These are areas in which ratios and other forms of quantifiable data cannot provide all the necessary information.

Interest rate risk. Farmers' State had a negative gap in 19X9 larger than the peer group. 19X9 was a year of falling interest rates, and the negative gap–holding more interest rate sensitive liabilities than assets–had a beneficial impact on Farmers' State's profits. Because of the heavy reliance on jumbo CD's mentioned above, it is likely that Farmers' State will continue to have a negative gap, which could prove problematic if interest rates rise.

Fraud risk. The percent of loans to insiders at Farmers'

State is low, indicating no apparent risk of fraud from this source.

Summary. Using the return on equity as an overall measure of bank performance, it would appear that Farmers' State is a well managed bank. In all but one year of the five-year period, the bank's return on equity has been well above the peer group average. Farmers' State has considerable risk but has managed that risk to advantage during the period. The strongest performance was in 19X5 when profits (as measured by return on assets) were at their highest levels. Part of the strong performance in 19X5, however, may have been due to inadequate loan loss provision, as was discussed above. One question raised in the analysis is whether the bank is in the same situation again in 19X9 given the huge increases in real estate loans.

The strength of this bank is its consistent ability to generate higher margins than its peers on interest-earning assets, particularly investments in securities, while controlling all areas of overhead expense and effectively managing risk. Farmers' State's return on equity provides ample evidence of the bank's managerial success. Major weaknesses are 1) the potential for higher loan losses in the future from real estate loans, 2) the historically high dividend payout ratio that inhibits internal capital growth, 3) possible problems with liquidity given the heavy reliance on volatile liabilities, 4) and a negative interest rate gap that could impair future profits if interest rates rise.

The analysis of Farmers' State bank provides an example of a small rural bank. The next section focuses on a large urban bank.

City National Bank

City National Bank is a metropolitan bank in a peer group that includes all insured commercial banks having assets in excess of $10 billion. Financial statements and key financial ratios for City National Bank are presented in Tables 5-4, 5-5, and 5-6.

Profitability. After four years of profit in 19X5 - 19X8, City National experienced a $77 million loss in 19X9. The peer group also reported an average loss for 19X9, though not as large as City National's (as measured by net income/average assets). Income on loans and leases at City National, while down from its banner year in 19X6, was higher in 19X9 than 19X8. City National's investment income has steadily risen since 19X6 to its highest level of the five-year period in 19X9. Why, then, the loss and what are the bank's prospects for the future?

The first step of any financial statement analysis should be a review of the income statement and balance sheet to note obvious trends and developments before beginning to look at the financial ratios. What leaps out of the City National Bank income statement as the major cause of the 19X9 loss is overhead expense which rose from $150 million in 19X8 to over $300 million in 19X9. Another major piece of analysis lies in the balance sheet account, "other real estate owned." Remember that the balance sheet is prepared at a point in time and some account balances, such as fed funds sold and purchased, can fluctuate dramatically from day-to-day. "Other real estate owned," however, would not be expected to fluctuate on a daily basis. The big increase in this account between 19X8 and 19X9 probably means that the bank has foreclosed on problem loans with real estate as collateral. Relating the huge increase in overhead expense to the jump in other real estate would indicate that City National is

Table 5-4
CITY NATIONAL BANK
BALANCE SHEET
Assets, Liabilities, and Capital ($000) at December 31,

Assets:		19x9	19X8	19X7	19X6	19X5
(1)	Real Estate Loans	1388673	1234627	1166254	1041079	394050
(2)	Commercial Loans	4322393	4568827	4498908	4759312	5099289
(3)	Individual Loans	269242	141691	150924	128107	113278
(4)	Agricultural Loans	82	0	0	0	0
(5)	Other LN & LS–Domestic	474947	589329	539637	550499	260515
(6)	LN & LS–Foreign	671680	700554	725618	791043	550161
(7)	Gross Loans & Leases	7127017	7235028	7081341	7270040	6417293
(8)	Less: Unearned Income	36948	24679	20045	20710	12922
(9)	Reserves	250095	189977	153868	73500	61940
(10)	Net Loans & Leases	6839974	7020372	6907428	7175830	6342431
(11)	U.S. Treas & Agen Securities	911056	1006876	477070	40933	399385
(12)	Municipal Securities	516248	458439	668639	498797	539281
(13)	Foreign Debt Securities	0	0	0	0	0
(14)	All Other Securities	295114	132112	11990	11988	12008
(15)	Int-Bearing Bank Bal.	600284	967152	1361615	1347633	1729276
(16)	Fed Funds Sold&Resales	265200	469185	473025	519315	624626
(17)	Trading Account Assets	1385	59277	30040	5907	2607
(18)	Total Investments	2589287	3093041	3022379	2792971	3307183
(19)	Total Earning Assets	9429261	10113413	9929807	9968711	9649714
(20)	Non-Int Cash, Due Fr Banks	1079325	936915	876990	1000920	1016117
(21)	Acceptances	37779	9954	396855	733890	802007
(22)	Prem, Fx Assets, Cap Leases	297037	211830	206088	198119	189806
(23)	Other Real Estate Owned	129845	59363	37771	35039	10376
(24)	Inv.Uncon.Subsidiaries	0	0	0	0	0
(25)	Other Assets	191405	177299	177654	205480	195079
(26)	Total Assets	11164652	11508704	11625165	12142159	11863099
(27)	Avg. Assets During Qtr.	10955681	10408474	10660677	11392078	10644303
Liabilities & Capital:						
(28)	Demand Deposits	2036266	1725136	1730266	1829157	1971407
(29)	All NOW & ATS Accounts	339018	159922	167723	108773	111697
(30)	MMDA Accounts	807038	409376	332526	273112	209927
(31)	Other Savings Deposits	176350	45224	45728	49621	57672
(32)	Nonbrok. Time Deps <$100M	686799	171377	161299	157529	134504
(33)	Core Deposits	405471	2511041	2437502	2418192	2485207
(34)	All Brokered Deposits	100813	259278	98972	45621	32211
(35)	Nonbrok. Time Deps >$100M	1512822	1467563	2451186	2216352	1529657
(36)	Deps in Foreign Offices	1068354	1369230	2064585	2095148	2196356
(37)	Total Deposits	6727460	5607112	7052245	6775310	6243431
(38)	Fed Funds Purch & Resale	3152466	4413945	2822917	2680541	3004198
(39)	Other Borrowings	413607	643017	524592	1100960	1112822
(40)	Volatile Liabilities	6248062	8153033	7962252	8138622	7875244
(41)	Accept.& Other Liabilities	207139	179019	580835	957572	961398
(42)	Total Liab. (Incl. Mtg)	10500672	10843093	10989918	11523772	11331286
(43)	Sub.Notes & Deben.	35000	35000	35000	35000	35000
(44)	All Common & Pfd Capital	628980	630611	600247	583387	496813
(45)	Total Liab. & Capital	11164652	11508704	11625165	12142159	11863099
Memoranda:						
(46)	Officer, Shholder Ln(#)	1	2	2	1	7
(47)	Officer, Shholder Ln ($)	16	93	101	81	897
(48)	Direct, Indirect Invest in RE	NA	NA	NA	NA	NA
(49)	Total Curr. Restruc. Debt	0	0	0	20	NA

133

Table 5-5
CITY NATIONAL BANK
INCOME STATEMENT
REVENUE AND EXPENSES ($000)
For Period ending December 31,

		19x9	19X8	19X7	19X6	19X5
(1)	Interest & Fees on loans	588292	567889	680030	802732	580643
(2)	Income from lease finc.	1723	2899	3800	4747	5648
(3)	Fully taxable	548213	564674	674586	799281	NA
(4)	Tax Exempt	5802	6114	9244	8198	NA
(5)	Estimated tax benefit	2127	5148	7839	7044	NA
(6)	Income on loans & leases (TE)	592142	575936	691669	814523	586291
(7)	U.S.Treas, agency securities	67987	55476	38481	49884	37451
(8)	Tax exempt security income	42264	37147	39300	29474	40789
(9)	Estimated tax benefit	15605	31623	33422	24976	34670
(10)	Other securities income	17827	1962	840	862	854
(11)	Invest. interest income (TE)	143683	126208	112043	105196	113764
(12)	Int. Fed funds sold,resales	31630	11942	23704	51394	42718
(13)	Int on due from banks	49341	84438	118134	127889	123443
(14)	Trading account income	2533	3634	1105	229	401
(15)	Total interest income (TE)	819330	802158	946656	1099232	866617
(16)	Interest on foreign deposits	74194	137125	171748	194725	161091
(17)	Interest on CD's over $100M	139895	148646	193534	190941	131648
(18)	Interest on other deposits	110632	54776	58920	64499	59954
(19)	Int on Fed funds purch/repos	197944	209140	233105	371094	255109
(20)	Interest borrowed money	34300	21232	32990	26216	20331
(21)	Int on mortgages & leases	1013	944	337	457	NA
(22)	Int on sub notes & debentures	3150	3150	3150	3150	3150
(23)	Total interest expense	561128	575013	693784	851082	631103
(24)	Net interest income (TE)	258202	227145	252872	248150	235514
(25)	Non-interest income	108770	86683	103504	56434	46360
(26)	Adjusted operating income (TE)	366972	313828	356376	304584	281874
(27)	Overhead expense	307221	149794	141883	119325	117136
(28)	Provision loan/lease loss	135487	115000	200000	39500	34300
(29)	Prov. allocated transfer risk	NA	NA	NA	NA	NA
(30)	Pretax operating income (TE)	-75735	48854	14493	145759	130438
(31)	Securities gains (losses)	45	23713	16929	14	86
(32)	Pretax net operating inc (TE)	-75690	72567	31422	145773	130524
(33)	Applicable income taxes	-16596	-14388	-31707	27178	13257
(34)	Current tax equiv adjustments	0	35976	0	32021	34670
(35)	Other tax equiv adjustments	17733	975	41262	0	0
(36)	Applicable income tax (TE)	1137	22383	9561	59199	47927
(37)	Net operating income	-76828	50364	21861	86574	82597
(38)	Net extraordinary items	0	0	0	0	0
(39)	Net income	-76828	50364	21861	86574	82597
(40)	Cash dividends declared	71229	20000	5000	0	0
(41)	Retained earnings	-148057	30364	16861	86574	82597
(42)	Memo: net int'l income	-49557	2782	5480	5556	-1789

Table 5-6
City National Bank

Financial Ratio (percent)	19X9 CNB	19X9 Peer	19X8 CNB	19X8 Peer	19X7 CNB	19X7 Peer	19X6 CNB	19X6 Peer	19X5 CNB	19X5 Peer
Profitability:										
(1) Net income/average assets	-0.70	-0.32	0.49	0.69	0.20	0.63	0.79	0.59	0.89	0.54
(2) Net interest income/average assets	2.36	3.06	2.21	3.25	2.32	3.21	2.26	2.85	2.54	2.79
(3) Non-interest income/average assets	1.00	1.47	0.84	1.34	0.95	1.22	0.51	1.12	0.50	0.95
(4) Overhead expense/average assets	2.81	2.99	1.46	2.82	1.30	2.72	1.08	2.47	1.26	2.35
(5) Provision for loan and lease losses/average assets	1.24	1.89	1.12	0.72	1.83	0.61	0.36	0.52	0.37	0.40
(6) Net securities gains or losses/average assets	0.00	0.07	0.23	0.13	0.16	0.07	0.00	0.01	0.00	0.01
(7) Net extraordinary items/average assets	0	0	0	0	0	0	0	0	0	0
(8) Applicable income taxes/average assets	0.01	0.24	0.22	0.58	0.09	0.50	0.54	0.42	0.52	0.39
(9) Interest income/average assets	7.50	8.05	7.81	8.51	8.68	9.37	9.99	10.29	9.35	9.43
(10) Interest expense/average assets	5.13	5.00	5.60	5.26	6.36	6.34	7.73	7.48	6.81	6.86
(11) Interest income/average earning assets	8.25	9.11	8.56	9.74	9.98	10.74	11.70	12.07	11.06	11.15
(12) Interest expense/average earning assets	5.65	5.62	6.14	6.03	7.32	7.23	9.06	8.84	8.06	7.88
(13) Personnel expense/average assets	1.20	1.45	0.98	1.43	0.87	1.39	0.81	1.30	0.89	1.25
(14) Occupancy expense/average assets	0.38	0.50	0.23	0.48	0.22	0.47	0.05	0.42	0.22	0.40
(15) Other operating expense/average assets	1.23	1.02	0.25	0.91	0.21	0.85	0.22	0.75	0.16	0.69
Capital Risk:										
(16) Primary capital/adjusted average assets	7.84	7.11	7.74	6.84	6.97	6.66	5.73	6.04	5.22	5.14
(17) Growth rate: assets	-2.99	3.64	-1.00	8.09	-4.26	7.01	2.35	3.84	16.78	2.26
(18) Growth rate: primary capital	6.99	11.70	8.81	10.84	14.80	14.69	17.56	21.25	19.43	9.05
(19) Cash dividends/net operating income	N A	97.33	39.71	42.60	22.87	38.99	0	41.40	0	46.37
Credit risk:										
(20) Net loss/total loans and leases	0.82	0.82	1.15	0.73	1.73	0.68	0.41	0.54	0.51	0.52
(21) Earnings coverage of net loss (X)	0.73	3.58	1.61	3.71	1.45	3.96	5.48	3.86	5.01	4.44
(22) Loss reserve/net loss (X)	4.32	5.48	2.41	2.73	1.29	3.14	2.63	2.66	2.38	2.77
(23) Loss reserve/total loans and leases	3.53	3.76	2.63	1.82	2.18	1.61	1.01	1.36	0.99	1.16
(24) Percent noncurrent loans and leases	7.62	4.25	6.26	2.77	4.49	2.78	2.20	3.54	3.53	4.00
(5) Provision loan loss/average assets	1.24	1.89	1.12	0.72	1.83	0.61	0.36	0.52	0.37	0.40
Liquidity:										
(25) Temporary investments/volatile liabilities	17.30	27.46	20.42	28.68	25.86	30.61	24.97	26.86	32.07	29.41
(26) Volatile liability dependence	61.89	51.07	76.80	50.65	75.00	51.70	76.94	56.23	75.09	60.11
(27) Loans and leases/assets	61.26	61.10	61.00	60.44	59.42	62.09	59.10	64.73	53.46	60.42
Interest rate:										
(28) Gap	-9.66	-7.37								
Fraud risk:										
(29) Officer, shareholder loans/assets	0	0.01	0	0.01	0	0	0	0	0	0
Summary										
(30) Net income/average equity	-12.36	-11.11	8.14	13.70	3.65	12.07	16.06	11.98	18.10	12.05

experiencing increased costs in managing foreclosed property from problem loans. This point underscores the importance of using the actual balance sheet and income statement numbers as well as the key financial ratios.

Another major cause of the 19X9 loss appears in the last line of the income statement showing net international income, an area in which City National experiences a net loss of about $50 million in 19X9, after reporting profit from foreign sources the other four years.

The analyst should note that while City National had a $77 million loss in 19X9, the bank paid over $71 million in cash dividends. The front cover of the Uniform Bank Performance Report indicates that City National is part of a holding company. It is apparent that the parent company has elected to take cash from City National in spite of its lack of income generation. In this situation the bank itself does not control the dividend payment although the bank's board may have some influence over dividend policy. Also, there are specific regulatory guidelines that affect cash dividend payments.

The financial ratios relating to profitability confirm the preliminary analysis begun with a review of the financial statements. City National has not outperformed its peer group since 19X6, and 19X9 was the worst year of the five-year period with a net income/assets of -0.70 compared with the peer group's -0.32. The bank's net interest income/assets is fairly constant over the period and, in fact, increased slightly between 19X8 and 19X9, but this ratio has consistently been lower than the peer group's. The five year trend reveals that City National receives less in net income than its peer group and pays more in interest. (Both interest expense and interest revenue have declined as the result of falling interest rates in the economy during 19X5 and 19X9.) The ratio of net loans and leases/assets (ratio 27) at City National is about the same as its peer group, and supplementary data (not shown here) in the Report indicate that City National earns less than the peer group on both loans-leases and investments and that its interest costs are greater on deposits. Some of the marginal disadvantage for City National may be regional since this bank, located in a southwestern state, is competing with the largest U.S. banks in the major money centers.

Non-interest income/assets for City has increased over the period–typical of banks in general since deregulation has resulted in more income from nontraditional services–but has been less than peer averages. The major source of difficulty for City National is overhead expense, which has jumped as a percentage of total assets from 1.46 to 2.81 between 19X8 and 19X9. This rise is largely attributed to costs associated with managing properties and other expenses relating to real estate repossessed from problem loans. Additional overhead expense is partly personnel but primarily in "other operating expense" (note the increase in that category relative to assets from .25 in 19X8 to 1.23 in 19X9) that would cover items such as taxes, insurance, and maintenance costs of the properties.

City National's provision for loan loss/average assets has increased substantially–from .37 in 19X5 to 1.24 in 19X9–contributing to declining profitability. Neither security transactions nor extraordinary items have been factors over the five year period. In summary, it would appear that profitability at City National has been severely impacted by problem loans and losses on foreign country operations.

Capital risk. Assets have declined at City National since 19X6, while primary capital has increased, but at decreasing rates. Until 19X9 City National retained about sixty percent of earnings. As mentioned above, City National's parent company was responsible for a substantial payment of dividends by City National in spite of the bank's loss for 19X9. Growth in primary capital for that year apparently resulted from the increase in reserve for loan and lease losses. It is impossible, as mentioned previously, to trace other changes in the equity account, such as transactions in the stock accounts, from the data provided in the Uniform Bank Performance Report. The ratio of primary capital to average assets would indicate a slight lessening of overall capital risk as the ratio has steadily increased over the period.

Credit risk. City National has major problems in the area of credit risk. Costs associated with uncollectible loans have already adversely affected profits (see above discussion of overhead expense). The percent of noncurrent loans and leases at City National has increased markedly since 19X6 and is substantially greater than the peer group. City National's earnings coverage of net loan and lease losses has also deteriorated and is well below the peer averages. The bank's loss reserve to net loss and loss reserve to total loans and leases indicates that the bank is building reserves to cover losses. The reserve to net losses has not grown apace with the peer group, raising questions about adequacy given the relatively high percentage of noncurrent loans. It is apparent that this bank has serious difficulties ahead with respect to loan collections.

Liquidity. City National's ratio of loans and leases to assets is roughly comparable to its peer group, but the bank's volatility dependence is much greater and its ratio of temporary investments to volatile liabilities is lower. City National depends more heavily than its peers on unstable funding sources–monies that could dry up quite rapidly–indicating that the bank has a potential for serious liquidity problems. A liquidity "red flag" from City National's balance sheet is the bank's increasing reliance on "brokered deposits" between 19X5 and 19X8. Banks turn to brokered deposits when other funding sources are not available. On the plus side, volatility dependence at City National, while high relative to the peer group, has been steadily decreasing since 19X6. Much of the decline has resulted from the reductions of deposits at foreign offices, considered among the least stable of all liabilities classified as "volatile." Given the overall loss from international exposure in 19X9, this reduction is probably a positive one. In general, the liquidity risk, while potentially serious for City National, appears to be lessening.

Interest rate risk. City National has a gap that is both negative and greater than its peer group. This negative gap contributed positively to income during 19X9, a year of declining interest rates, but will have the reverse effect if interest rates rise. Since the gap is calculated at a point in time–in this case the end of the year–City National may have the capacity to change its magnitude and direction in the short-term, thereby reducing interest rate risk.

Fraud risk. There is no evidence of any fraud risk from officer and shareholder loans at City National, as these loans account for less than .00 percent of total assets.

Summary. City National Bank had a negative return on equity in 19X9 and has experienced, overall, decreasing returns since 19X5. The return on equity is the combined result of problems in generating profits, and the management of risk, especially credit risk. City National's return on assets has been lower than the peer group since 19X6, and profits were negative in 19X9. Additionally, neither the bank's net interest income nor non-interest income has kept pace with its peers. Increases in overhead expense associated with problem loans and the provision for loan losses have contributed heavily to decreasing returns, with little income from other sources to offset the added costs. The level of primary capital to assets has increased over the period, indicating a reduction in overall risk, but the growth in primary capital has been largely the result of additions to the loans loss reserve to provide for potential problem loans. Credit risk will apparently continue to be the major problem for City National, given the high and rising proportion of noncurrent loans. The bank's liquidity situation has improved recently, but City National continues to have an above-average reliance on volatile liabilities, including brokered deposits, which could lead to funding problems. On balance, the performance weaknesses at City National far outweigh the strengths at this point. The critical issue will be City National's ability to manage its credit risk.

Conclusion

The evaluations of Farmers' State, a small rural bank, and City National, a large metropolitan bank, have been presented to provide examples of how to approach the analysis of banking performance and make conclusions based on data drawn from a bank's Uniform Bank Performance Report. The evaluation of banking performance requires an understanding of the institution's balance sheet, income statement, key financial ratios, and peer group data. The objective of a performance analysis is to evaluate the bank's ability to generate profits to its owners through effective risk management. Although each situation will be different, depending on the characteristics and record of the bank under review, the approach presented in Chapters 3, 4, and 5 will apply to any insured commercial banking institution in the United States.

6

Predicting Bank Financial Distress and Failure

Previous chapters have provided an overview of the various dimensions of bank performance and the financial ratios designed to provide measurement of that performance. Internal and external (shareholders, depositors, and other creditors) analysts should find these financial ratios useful in their evaluation of bank performance. The emphasis has been on using the data provided in the Uniform Bank Performance Report to obtain a complete picture of a commercial bank's financial performance. This data allows an analyst to determine the reasons for a bank's high or low performance in relation to its peer group. Perhaps the performance is due to lending policy or a particular asset/liability management or to control of overhead expenses. Discussion in the previous chapters enabled the analyst to piece together the puzzle to discover answers to a variety of important questions concerning bank performance.

The present chapter is narrower in focus in that it concentrates on explaining and predicting the financial condition of floundering and failing banks. Specifically, it surveys and evaluates the extensive literature that has attempted to find variables useful in predicting bank financial distress and failure. Not only is identification of such variables potentially valuable to uninsured depositors and other creditors who are "at risk," but such an analysis allows analysts to select the financial ratios that are most important.

In using financial variables to identify floundering and failing banks, it must be recognized that the potential for fraud as a cause of failure tempers the usefulness of these ratios. As discussed earlier, a considerable number of bank failures involve fraud either as the principal or supporting cause. To the extent that the fraudulent activities of officers, directors, and others in the bank are not reflected in the financial statements prior to the event, the financial ratio data will not be useful in predicting financial distress.

Models used by bank regulatory authorities to identify financial ratios that are usable in identifying banks that would become problems *prior* to the time that these problems become evident are discussed at the beginning of this chapter. This is followed by an explanation of the financial ratios that various analysts have found important in predicting bank distress and failure. Also included is a discussion of the uses of stock and bond price data from the capital markets as a means of predicting financial distress.

Models developed to distinguish between problem and nonproblem banks are often referred to as "Early Warning Systems" while those developed to distinguish between failed and nonfailed banks are referred to as "Failure Prediction Models." Both approaches are discussed here. Although many of these models include complex statistical procedures, this discussion focuses on the important variables without treating in detail their statistical approaches, results, and limitations. For additional information, refer to the original publications listed in the references section at the end of the book.

Variables Used By Regulators.

Table 6-1 shows some of the important financial ratios that have been used by the three federal bank regulatory agencies in their early warning systems. (While the variables change over time, most of the dimensions of bank performance discussed earlier in the book are included in the list.) The purpose of early warning systems is to reduce a large number of financial ratios to a summary set that individually and taken together provide a useful indicator of future problems at individual commercial banks. Taken as a group, the variables produce a composite score or rating for the individual bank that can be used by bank regulators to adjust their on-site evaluation of the institution. Ratios are grouped together according to the various aspects of bank performance, including those related to capital, profitability, asset quality, liquidity, interest sensitivity and liabilities for borrowed money, efficiency ratios, change ratios, etc. As displayed in the table, different regulators have used different ratios in their analysis. Also, the FDIC used critical values of the variables (designated as "C") while the Federal Reserve and the Office of the Controller of the Currency (OCC) used composite scores in their screening.

The Federal Reserve employed just nine variables in its early warning model, including two capital ratios. The FDIC employed eight ratios, though there was a slight difference in their composition. The OCC used eleven variables, including three that measured the rate of change in the portfolio of the bank.

The importance of both capital and profitability is suggested by these three early warning system models. The three regulatory agencies have included two capital ratios in their model. Moreover, each one except the Federal Reserve has employed two (or more) variables designed to capture profitability.

TABLE 6-1

FINANCIAL RATIOS USED BY FEDERAL BANK REGULATORS IN EARLY WARNING SYSTEMS

Financial Ratio	Federal Regulator		
	FRB	FDIC	OCC
Capital			
(1) Equity capital decrease		X	
(2) Equity capital/Total assets		C	X
(3) Retained earnings/ Average equity capital			X
(4) Equity capital/ Adjusted equity capital	X		
(5) Gross capital/ Adjusted risk assets	X		
Profitability			
(1) Net Operating income/ Average total assets		C	
(2) Net income/Assets			X
(3) Interest expense on deposits and federal funds purchased and borrowings/Total operating income		C	
(4) Adjusted return on assets			X
(5) Net income/ Total assets-cash items	X		X
(6) Total other earnings/ Average assets			X
Asset Quality			
(1) Gross loan losses/Net operating income + Provision	X		
(2) Provision for possible loan losses/Average assets			X
(3) Gross charge-offs - Recoveries/Average loans		C	

TABLE 6-1 (continued)

Financial Ratio	Federal Regulator		
	FRB	FDIC	OCC
Liquidity			
(1) Net borrowings - Mortgages/Cash and due from banks + Total securities maturing in one year or less		C	
Interest Sensitivity and Liabilities for Borrowed Money			
(1) $100,000 or more time deposits + Net borrowings/Total loans		C	
(2) Interest-sensitive funds/ Total sources of funds	X		
Efficiency Ratios			
(1) Total operating expenses/ Total operating income	X		
(2) Non-interest expense/ Total operating income – Interest expense	X		
(3) Net interest earnings/ Average assets			X
Change Ratios			
(1) Change in asset mix			X
(2) Change in liability mix			X
(3) Change in loan mix			X
(4) Cash dividends on common and preferredstock/Net income		C	
(5) Cash dividends/Net Income	X		
Other Ratios			
(1) Commercial and industrial loans/ Total loans, gross	X		

Source: Barron H. Putnam, "Early Warning Systems and Financial Analysis in Bank Monitoring," *Federal Reserve Bank of Atlanta Economic Review,* (November 1983): 9-10.

Examination of these early warning systems indicates four primary determinants of financial soundness for a banking organization:

(1) Earnings

(2) Liquidity

(3) Asset Quality

(4) Capital Adequacy

How might the analyst use the variables developed from the Early Warnings System models? Using the model employed by the FDIC as an example, what might cause the analyst to be concerned about the financial performance of a banking organization? Certainly a decrease in equity capital would be of concern as would a ratio of equity capital to total assets that is below some critical level (such as below the average for the peer group). But what might cause equity capital to decline and fall below that critical level? There are two principal factors. First, the bank may be experiencing operating losses–which reduces equity capital dollar for dollar through the effects on retained earnings. The FDIC, therefore, included a profitability measure in its early warning system–the ratio of net operating earnings to total assets. But a bank may experience declining equity capital and equity capital ratios even when highly profitable if it pays excessive amounts of cash dividends. Notice that the EWS ratio used by the FDIC was the change in the ratio of cash dividends on common and preferred stock to net income, a measure that should be closely related to the equity capital ratios.

The early warning system used by the FDIC incorporated principal measures of risk: capital asset quality, liquidity, interest sensitivity and liabilities for borrowed money risk. The capital measure was the change in total equity capital or in the ratio of equity capital to total assets. The asset quality measure was the ratio of net charge-offs on loans (gross charge-offs minus recoveries) to average loans. The liquidity measure was the ratio of net borrowings to cash and due from banks plus total securities maturing in one year or less. The interest sensitivity measure was the amount of jumbo time deposits plus net borrowings divided by the amount of total loans. Of course, increases in net charge-offs signal a cause for concern and represent an early warning signal of future financial distress. Similarly, reductions in liquidity due to greater reliance on net borrowings relative to highly liquid assets or in relation to loans are potential signals of future financial problems.

Variables Developed by Analysts

In a sense, early warning systems models are failure prediction models and analysts can use these financial ratios to forecast the financial distress or failure of a banking organization. Failure prediction models are those used to focus directly on the probability of failure.

There have been numerous early warning system and failure prediction models developed by analysts from the private sector as well as those employed by the bank regulatory agencies. These models differ greatly in the exact variables used and the various statistical tests employed. Results, however, suggest that financial ratio data are useful and important in distinguishing between problem and nonproblem banks and failed and nonfailed banks and that only a relatively small set of financial statement ratios are needed in these models. The following overview, though not exhaustive, does provide insight into the nature of the variables and the models used.

Early Studies

Table 6-2 provides a set of financial ratios that have been important in a number of studies that attempted to predict financial distress and failure. Some of the ratios were developed for use by the bank regulatory authorities (and contributed to the Early Warning Systems discussed above) while others reflect the results of academic research studies. As would be expected, there is substantial commonality among the variables, at least in terms of the dimensions of bank performance that the studies examined.

A brief discussion of some of the ratios used in these studies may provide some insight into the important dimensions of failure prediction models. In an early (1974) study of bank failure prediction models, Stuhr and Van Wicklen used standard financial ratios similar to those discussed above (as shown in Table 6-1), variables which captured the quality of assets, capital, income, loans, and expenses.[1] The asset quality measure–the ratio of classified and special mention assets to bank capital–would not usually be available to external analysts; internal bank analyses such as those done by senior management, would have access to that information. At about the same time, Joseph Sinkey developed a model designed to differentiate between problem and nonproblem banks.[2] The variables used were traditional measures of liquidity, loan volume, loan quality, capital adequacy, efficiency, and sources of revenue. As shown in Table 6-2, the

---

1. David Stuhr, and Robert Van Wicklen, "Rating and Financial Condition of Banks: A Statistical Approach to Aid Bank Supervision," *Federal Reserve Bank of New York Monthly Review*, (September 1974): 233-238.

2. Joseph Sinkey, "A Multivariate Statistical Analysis of the Characteristics of Problem Banks," *The Journal of Finance*, (March 1975): 21-38.

TABLE 6-2
Financial Ratios Identified in Early Warning and Failure Prediction Models

David Stuhr and
Robert Van Wicklen
- Asset quality (ratio of classified and special mentioned assets to bank capital)
- Capital adequacy (capital to assets)
- Management (three variables were used, the most important of which were net operating income to assets and a debt to equity ratio)
- Asset size of bank
- Net occupancy expense to net income
- Loans to total assets ratio

Joseph Sinkey
- Liquidity
- Loan volume
- Loan quality
- Capital adequacy
- Efficiency
- Sources of revenue

Daniel Martin
- Net income to total assets (earnings variable)
- Gross charge-offs to net operating income (asset quality)
- Expenses to operating revenues
- Loans to total assets
- Commercial loans to total loans (risk variable)
- Gross capital to risk assets (capital adequacy)

Korobow, Stuhr and Martin
- Loans and leases to total sources of funds (liquidity variable)
- Equity capital to adjusted risk assets (capital adequacy)
- Operating expense to operating revenues (income variable)
- Gross charge-offs to net income plus provisions for loan losses (asset quality)
- Commercial and industrial loans to total loans (risk variable)

Source: Barron H. Putnam, "Early Warning Systems and Financial Analysis in Bank Monitoring," *Federal Reserve Bank of Atlanta Economic Review*, (November 1983): 13.

variables used by Martin[3] and Korobow, Stuhr, and Martin[4] were similar to those used in the two studies just discussed.

Predicting Financial Distress and Failure Since Deregulation

As pointed out throughout this book, the environment within which banks operate has changed dramatically in recent years. Bank management practices have also changed, including the willingness of banks to accept greater degrees of risk. This raises the question of the validity of previous studies of bank financial ratios as used to predict financial distress and failure in the dynamic market environment of the 1990s. One recent study addressed that question.[5] It finds that,

> ..specific bank failures can be predicted fairly accurately, well in advance of failure, even when the basis for these predictions is limited to publicly available information...the principal cause of bank failure remains the same as in earlier decades, namely poor bank management, resulting in excessive risk-taking or a lack of controls that permits fraud and embezzlement.

This study considered ratios designed to measure the profitability of the banking organization, management efficiency, leverage, risk/diversification, and economic variables of the market area in which the bank operated. These

---

3. Daniel Martin, "Early Warnings of Bank Failure: A Logit Regression Approach," *Journal of Banking and Finance*, (November,1977): 249-277

4. Leon Korobow, David Stuhr, and David Martin," A Nationwide Test of Early Warning Research in Banking, *Federal Reserve Bank of New York Quarterly Review*, (Autumn 1977): 37-52

5. Colleen Pantalone and Marjorie Platt, "Predicting Commercial Bank Failure Since Deregulation," *Federal Reserve Bank of Boston New England Economic Review*, (July/August 1987): 37-46.

variables are shown in Table 6-3. An attempt was made to predict the 1983 and 1984 failures of 113 commercial banks using these data for each six-month period up to twenty-four months prior to failure.

The ratios shown in Table 6-3 were simplified into the following five which appeared to be most significantly related to the probability of failure:

1. net income to total assets
2. equity capital to total assets
3. total loans to total assets
4. commercial loans to total assets
5. the absolute value of the percentage change in residential construction.

Of the financial variables, the ratios of net income to total assets and equity capital to total assets were both positively related to the financial health of commercial banks. This is not surprising. A healthy bank generates operating earnings which are useful in increasing the equity base of the organization. By contrast, the other financial variables–total loans to total assets (a measure of liquidity risk) and commercial and industrial loans to total assets (a measure of diversification)–were negatively related to financial health. Banks that made more loans (and held less securities) were more likely to fail. Similarly, banks that made more commercial and industrial (i.e., business) loans, and hence were not well diversified, were more likely to fail. It is interesting and important to note that these variables are similar to those found in other studies of bank failures.

In another recent study, Whalen and Thompson[6] attempt to predict a bank's CAMEL (Capital adequacy, Asset quality,

6. Gary Whalen and James B. Thompson, "Using Financial Data to Identify Changes in Bank Condition," *Federal Reserve Bank of Cleveland Economic Review*, (2nd Quarter, 1988): 17-26.

TABLE 6-3

Ratios Considered in Predicting Bank Failure Since Deregulation

Profitability
- Net income/total assets*
- Net income/equity capital

Management Efficiency
- Interest expense/total liabilities
- Interest on deposits/net income
- Compensation/total expense
- Occupancy expense/total expense

Leverage
- Equity capital/total assets*
- Long-term debt/equity capital

Risk/Diversification
- Total loans/total assets*
- Commercial and industrial loans/total loans*
- Real estate loans/total loans
- Consumer loans/total loans
- Agricultural loans/total loans
- RPs and federal funds purchased/total assets
- RPs and federal funds sold/total assets

State Economic Variables (absolute values)
- Percentage change in disposable personal income
- Percentage change in residential construction*
- Percentage change in unemployment
- Percentage change in population

*Variables selected as best predictors of bank failures

Source: Colleen C. Pantalone and Marjorie B. Platt, "Predicting Commercial Bank Failure Since Deregulation," *Federal Reserve Bank of Boston New England Economic Review*, (July/August): 40.

Management, Earnings, and Liquidity) rating on its examination using financial ratio data. (CAMEL ratings fall between one, the lowest risk, and five, the highest risk.) The variables used in the analysis are given in Table 6-4. They include the variables often found to be important but with some unusual additions. For example, the study included the ratio of nonperforming loans to primary capital. It also made use of the gap, using the one year gap expressed both as a fraction of equity capital and total assets. Finally, the study used the ratio of brokered deposits to total deposits. Brokered deposits are usually considered to be highly volatile and are viewed as a risk measure since banks in financial distress frequently find it necessary to substitute brokered deposits for the other deposits which leave the bank as problems are identified.

Whalen and Thompson used these variables to attempt to classify fifty-eight banks by their CAMEL rating. They found classification ability comparable to that of other studies. Most importantly, they found that relatively simple models that use only a few variables derived solely from published financial data did a good job of explaining a bank's CAMEL rating. Asset quality and earnings measures appeared especially important.

The asset quality variable-nonperforming loans as a ratio to primary capital–appeared to be the dominant variable. As the authors pointed out,

> Particularly noteworthy is the performance of the asset-quality proxy, non-performing loans divided by primary capital. Models employing only this variable perform as well as more complicated models. (p. 24)

In a related study using data since deregulation, Barth, Brumbaugh, Sauerhaft and Wang attempt to identify the

TABLE 6-4

Variables Used By Whalen and Thompson

Ratio Number	Definition
1	Primary capital/average assets
2	Payout ratio
3	Asset growth rate
4	Net loan and lease charge-offs/average total loans and leases
5	Current recoveries/prior charge-offs
6	Nonperforming loans and leases/primary capital
7	Loans and leases, past due and nonaccrual/ gross loans and leases
8	Loan loss reserve/total loans and leases
9	Return on average assets
10	Adjusted return on average assets
11	Pretax return on average assets
12	Net interest margin
13	Overhead expense/average earning assets
14	Provision for loan losses/average earning assets
15	Securities gains or losses/average earning assets
16	One year GAP/equity capital
17	One year GAP/total assets
18	Average earning assets/interest bearing liabilities
19	Loans plus securities/total sources of funds
20	Volatile liabilities/total sources of funds
21	Net funds dependency
22	Brokered deposits/total deposits

Source: Gary Whalen and James B. Thomson, "Using Financial Data to Identify Changes in Bank Condition," *Federal Reserve Bank of Cleveland Economic Review*, (2nd Quarter, 1988): 20.

variables that are useful in predicting the failure of 319 savings and loans from December 1981 through December 1987.[7] They selected twelve variables similar to those used in previous failure prediction models and classified those variables into six categories: (1) capital adequacy, (2) profitability, (3) credit risk, (4) interest rate risk, (5) liquidity and (6) other.

The results of the study are similar to the studies of bank failure prediction. As the authors pointed out,

> ...only a few key variables are necessary to provide significant explanatory power for determining the likelihood of thrift institution failures. (p. 20)

In fact, the best prediction of savings and loan failure using data six months before failure included only four variables: the ratio of net worth to total assets, the ratio of net income to total assets, the ratio of liquid assets to total assets and the total assets of the institution.

In another study using recent data, Peterson and Scott examine the causes of bank failures in the period from 1983 through the first quarter of 1984.[8] They studied the influence of financial performance as well as fraud for a group of forty-seven banks that failed during this period. A comparison of the financial data on the forty-seven banks that failed with that of similar-sized banks is given in Table 6-5. The failed banks are compared with peer group banks in section 1 of the table, with regard to their return on assets (ROA), their equity/assets ratio (E/A), their ratios of net charge-offs to

---

7. Joseph Barth, R. Dan Brumbaugh, Daniel Sauerhaft, and George Wang, "Thrift-Institution Failures: Causes and Policy Issues," Federal Reserve Bank of Chicago, *Proceedings of a Conference on Bank Structure and Competition,* (May 1-3, 1985): 184-216.

8. R. Peterson and W. Scott, "Major Causes of Bank Failures," Federal Reserve Bank of Chicago, *Proceedings of a Conference on Bank Structure and Competition,* (May 1-3, 1985): 166-183.

total assets, and the net interest margin (NIM), not only for the most recent year before failure but also for previous years.

Differences between the profitability and equity positions of the failed and peer group banks are striking. Thirty-five of the forty-seven banks had below average ROA in the year prior to failure while forty-two had equity capital ratios that were below average. In contrast, failure did not appear to be the result of excessively high net charge-offs, low net interest margins, or high overhead. In fact, the net interest margin for the failed banks was above average for thirty-one of the banks one year before failure and for twenty-five of the failed banks two years before failure, perhaps reflecting the large amounts of risk in the portfolio of the failed banks.

The data in this study are consistent with the argument that bank failures are associated with excessively rapid growth in the period immediately preceding failure (sometimes called the "Rapid Growth" syndrome). In fact, thirty-six of the forty-seven failed banks had total asset growth exceeding twenty percent in the year prior to failure. Similar results existed for time and savings deposit growth and growth in other liabilities in the year prior to failure.

Peterson and Scott also examined the association between bank failures and fraud as revealed in a U.S. government study of malfeasance at commercial banks.[9] They found that many of the failures in which banks had low ROAs as well as failures in which banks had excessively rapid asset growth involved malfeasance.

---

9. See: House of Representatives, Federal response to *Criminal Misconduct By Bank Officers, Directors and Insiders*, (Part I) 98th Congress, 1st Session, (June 28, 1983), *Federal Response to Criminal Misconduct by Bank Officers, Directors, and Insiders*, (Part II). 98th Congress, 2nd Session, (May 2, 1982).

TABLE 6-5
KEY RATIOS AND GROWTH TRENDS
OF FAILED BANKS

47 Commercial Bank Failures in 1983 & 1984

	# below average or low	# above average or high
I. Ratios relative to similar-size banks		
ROA-1	35	12
ROA-2	36	11
Equity/Asset-1	42	5
Equity/Asset-2	39	8
Equity/Asset-3	36	11
Net Charge-Offs/Loans-1	9	38
Net Charge-Offs/Loans-2	23	24
NIM-1	31	16
NIM-2	25	22
II. Overhead to Asset	Low	High
Ratios	(<3%)	(>5%)
Overhead-1	6	22
Overhead-2	8	16
III. Growth Exceeded		
20% in:	No	Yes
Total Assets-1	36	11
Total Assets-2	36	12
Time & Savings Deposits-1	32	15
Time & Savings Deposits-2	26	21
Other Liabilities-1	36	7
Other Liabilities-2	10	32

Because of data limitations, not all variables were observed for each failed bank.

The suffix 1 refers to the reporting year immediately prior to failure;

The suffix 2 refers to the reporting year before that.

Source: Richard L. Peterson and William L. Scott, "Major Causes of Bank Failures," Federal Reserve Bank of Chicago, *Proceedings of a Conference on Bank Structure and Competition*, (May 1-3, 1985): 81.

In summary, Peterson and Scott concluded:

> Overall the data indicate that most bank failures in 1982, 1983, and 1984 were associated either with malfeasance, sustained low performance, or excessive uncontrolled growth. (p. 174)

Sinkey[10] provides historical perspective by comparing the characteristics of large bank failures in the 1970s with those in the early 1980s. The failures included, in the 1970s, Bank of the Commonwealth (1972), United States National of San Diego (1973), Franklin National (1974), Security National (1975), and Hamilton National (1976). In the 1980s, the study included First Pennsylvania (1980), First National Bank of Midland (1983) and United American Bank (1983).

Sinkey found that, for the 1970s group, the return on equity (ROE) of these banks was below the norm even 3.5 years prior to failure. Moreover, the ROE's were deteriorating. Why did the banks earn less on equity for many years prior to their failure? Sinkey discovered a number of reasons. First, and not surprisingly, the banks made a large number of bad loans; their ratios of nonperforming loans and loan losses were quite high. Second, and particularly interesting, the banks had experienced major changes in their corporate strategies, some of which involved taking on additional interest rate risk.

By the 1980s, the economic and regulatory environment had changed dramatically. Interest rates were much more volatile and Congress had passed two major pieces of legislation to deregulate the industry. But these banks failed for traditional reasons–bad loans, rapid growth, taking on excessive interest rate risk, judgment errors and, in some cases, dishonesty.

---

10. Joseph Sinkey, The Characteristics of Large and Failed Banks," *Issues in Bank Regulation*, (Winter 1985): 43-50.

What can be learned from these major problem and failed banks? Sinkey points to the basic rules that allow banks to avoid failure:

> Don't make too many bad loans and don't bet the bank on interest rate movements.

Using Capital Market Data

Another approach to identifying those banks which are likely to become problems and even to fail is to make use of capital market information on stock and bond market prices. Following the Efficient Market Hypothesis (EMH), the prices of stocks and bonds should adjust instantly to all new information relevant to the risk and return of the securities. If, as seems to be the case, the financial ratios of banks that are about to become troubled or to fail deteriorate over some considerable time, it would be expected that the prices of the stocks and bonds of these banks would fall well in advance of their financial distress.

While appealing in concept, the usefulness of capital market data to anticipate bank financial problems is limited by the fact that only a few hundred of the many thousands of U.S. commercial banks have publicly traded securities. These are usually the largest banks and bank holding companies, so analysts interested in predicting financial distress at small and medium-sized banks are unlikely to be able to use this approach. In addition, studies of the ability of capital market data to anticipate bank failures are by no means consistent.

Shick and Sherman examined the usefulness of a model using bank stock prices to predict problems at twenty-five

---

11. Richard Shick and Lawrence Sherman, "Bank Stock Prices as an Early Warning System of Changes in Condition," *Journal of Bank Research*, (Autumn 1980): 136-146.

large U.S. banks. They found a significant decline in bank stock prices more than a year before the problems were uncovered through the examination process.[11] Relatedly, Stover and Miller found that the money market had anticipated the failure of Franklin National Bank, but the timing of the capital market adjustment was very close to the failure date, thereby severely limiting the usefulness of the capital market information.[12] Using equity market data, Pettway found that prices for the equity of seven large banks that failed during the 1972-1976 period adjusted well in advance of the failure.[13] However, in a related study of the failures of six large banks during the 1970s, Simpson found no evidence that stock prices accurately anticipated the event.[14] Given these conflicting results as well as the lack of data available for most banks, the usefulness of capital market data in predicting bank financial distress and failure may remain quite limited.

Perhaps the most comprehensive study of the ability of the market to anticipate problems at banking organizations was done at the Federal Reserve Bank of Boston.[15] In this study, Richard Randall examined each bank holding company with total assets over $2 billion that became a "problem" in the period from 1980 through mid 1987. The criteria for a problem bank were: (a) return on assets of under 0.5 percent for

12. Roger Stover and James Miller, "Additional Evidence on the Capital Market Effect of Bank Failures," *Financial Management*, (Spring 1983): 36-41.

13. Richard Pettway, "The Effects of Large Bank Failures Upon Investors' Risk Cognizance in the Commercial Banking Industry," *Journal of Financial and Quantitative Analysis*, (September 1976): 465-477.

14. W. Gary Simpson, "Capital Markets Prediction of Large Commercial Bank Failures An Alternative Analysis," *The Financial Review*, (February 1983): 33-55.

15. Richard E. Randall, "Can the Market Evaluate Asset Quality Exposure in Banks?" *Federal Reserve Bank of Boston New England Economic Review*, (July/August 1989): 3-24.

a calendar year; (b) ratio of net losses to loans of 1.3 percent or more for a calendar year or (c) a ratio of nonperforming assets to loans of 4.0 percent or more at any year end. This resulted in a sample of forty bank holding companies of which nine are money centers or large regional banking organizations. Nineteen were located in the Southwest.

The Randall study attempted to determine whether the market failed to recognize and discount the problems as they developed, and until significant, perhaps fatal damage, was done. The evidence presented was of two types:

(1) The behavior of the prices of individual stocks both absolutely and as compared to selected indices.

(2) The observations of bank stock analysts and changes in ratings at the debt rating services.

After evaluating this evidence, the author concluded:

> The evidence of this study is that neither the stock market nor the bank rating agencies identified problems in large BHC's in the 1980s until after substantial damage had been done. Furthermore, neither was able to correctly evaluate the seriousness of credit problems even when they had been identified. (p.18)

Bank Location, Bank Size, and Failure Risk

It is sometimes argued that another approach to predicting financial distress and failure involves concentrating on those banks that operate in geographical areas that are experiencing economic difficulty or on relatively small banks. The logic behind this argument is relatively simple: with regard to geographic location, since banks usually gather their deposits from a relatively small geographical area and make their loans within that same area, the ability of bank to grow through attracting core deposits and to collect their loans depends upon the economic health of the market areas they serve. Banks prosper when their community prospers and fail when their community's economy deteriorates. The experience of banks in the energy states and those serving agricultural areas in the mid to late 1980s is often cited to support this argument.

The size/failure correlation is based upon the premise that small banks are unable to achieve a diversified loan portfolio. Hence, when the economy they serve suffers, the loss rate on their portfolio increases, sometimes dramatically, and financial distress and failure often follow. Additionally, small banks often have less sophisticated management. As a result, dealing with asset/liability management and complex issues concerning the latest computer technology may be difficult for some of the smaller banks.

While location and size factors are not, by themselves, sufficient to allow the analyst to pick individual banks that are likely to fail, they at least provide a starting point for analysis. But are location and size actually related to failure? Evidence to date on the location/failure relationship appears stronger than that of the size/failure relationship.

Table 6-6 provides a classification of 1987 bank failures classified by state, by whether the failed bank was an agricultural bank (defined as a bank having twenty-five percent or more of its total loan portfolio consisting of farm loans), and by the total asset size of the bank. The association between the location of the bank and failure seems rather clear from the evidence in this table. More than one-half of the total number of bank failures (eighty-one of 150) took place in only three, energy-dependent, states: Louisiana, Oklahoma, and Texas. Forty-five of these failures were at agricultural banks, while thirty-three were at agricultural banks which were not located in the three energy-dependent states.

TABLE 6-6
1987 BANK FAILURE BY STATE
As of October 30, 1987

	Failed Banks	Assets ($ million)
Alabama	2	$ 24.4
Alaska	1	214.9
California	8	250.0
Colorado	11	166.7
Florida	3	259.7
Illinois	2	31.9
Indiana	3	80.4
Iowa	5	80.4
Kansas	6	176.0
Louisiana	8	519.2
Massachusetts	2	577.3
Minnesota	10	134.3
Mississippi	1	14.6
Missouri	4	50.6
Montana	3	38.8
Nebraska	2	36.0
New York	1	178.8
North Dakota	2	23.9
Ohio	1	8.7
Oklahoma	29	873.9
Pennsylvania	1	12.5
South Dakota	1	21.2
Texas	44	1,768.0
Utah	3	55.3
Wyoming	3	146.6
TOTAL	156	$5,744.1

*Defined as a bank having 25 percent or more of its total loan portfolio consisting of farm loans.

DISTRIBUTION OF FAILED BANKS BY ASSET SIZE
($ millions)
(October 30, 1987)

Total	≤25	25<50	50<100	100<300
156	116	23	8	9

Source: FDIC Regulatory Review, September/October 1987, p. 51.

The association between size and failure is not as easy to determine. As shown at the bottom of Table 6-6, small banks accounted for most of the failures. In fact, 110 of the 156 failures took place at banks with less than $25 million in total assets. But the fact that there are more small than large banks confounds the attempt to associate bank size with failure.

The real question is whether the failure rate is greater for small banks than for large banks. On this question, there is a lack of agreement in existing literature. Rose and Scott find that small rural banks are more likely to fail than large banks or small urban banks. Generally,[16] those failures took place in states that limited or prohibited branch banking. In contrast, however, Whitehead and Schweitzer find that, when all types of risk are examined (not just credit risk), the risk of small banks is no greater than the risk of large banks.[17]

Summary and Conclusions

While the characteristics of the banks studied in this chapter vary, they have enough commonality to allow a number of conclusions to be drawn. First, despite the potential problems created in using financial ratios due to the existence of fraud as a cause of bank failures, it does appear that financial ratios such as those contained in the Uniform Bank Performance Report are useful in predicting bank financial distress and failure. Indeed, the financial ratios of distressed and failed banks appear to deteriorate well in advance of the time when the severity of the problems are recognized. Second, problem and failed banks can be identi-

16. Peter Rose and William Scott, "Risk in Commercial Banking: Evidence from Postwar Failures," *Southern Economic Journal*, (July 1978): 90-106.

17. David Whitehead and Robert Schweitzer, "Bank Size and Risk: A Note on the Evidence," *Federal Reserve Bank of Atlanta Economic Review*, (November 1982): 32-34.

fied with a relatively simple set of financial ratios. While more complex models with more variables may increase the ability to identify problem banks, models that use a few variables seem to do well enough to be practicable for the analyst. Third, the variables used to identify these problem institutions are basic financial ratio measures such as profitability and capital adequacy ratios, which are easily accessible to the practicing analyst

It thus appears that a depositor, creditor, stockholder, internal analyst or other interested party could easily track the chances of failure of a particular bank by selecting a few basic variables and monitoring them closely. Deterioration in these variables would strongly indicate deterioration in the financial condition of the bank and signify concern over future failure. And the signal would come in ample time to allow for deposit withdrawal or other actions. Although the variables are not perfect and will sometimes give false signals, they appear accurate enough to be employed by those interested in monitoring their bank's performance.

References

A. Books

Austin, D., D. Hakala, and T. Scampini. *Modern Banking*, Boston: Bankers Publishing Co., 1985, Ch. 5.

Crumbley, D., N. Apostolou, and G. Simonton. *Handbook of Financial Management for Commercial Banks*, New York: McGraw-Hill, 1988.

Federal Reserve Bank of New York. *Recent Trends in Commercial Bank Profitability*, New York, 1986.

Fraser, L.M. *Understanding Financial Statements*, Second Edition, Englewood Cliffs, NJ: Prentice-Hall, 1988.

Garcia, F. *How to Analyze a Bank Statement*, Boston: Bankers Publishing Co., 1974.

Graddy, D., A. Spencer, and W. Brunsen. Commercial Banking and the Financial Services Industry, Reston, Virginia: Reston Publishing Co., 1985, Chs. 9 and 10.

Gunther, Jeffery W. *Texas Banking Conditions: Managerial Versus Economic Conditions*, Federal Reserve Bank of Dallas, October 1989.

Gup, B., D. Fraser, and J. Kolari. *Commercial Bank Management*, New York: John Wiley and Sons, 1989, Ch. 3.

Hays, D. *Bank Funds Management*, Ann Arbor, Michigan: University of Michigan Press, 1980.

Hempel, G., A. Coleman, and D. Simonson. *Bank Management: Text and Cases*, New York: John Wiley and Sons, 1986, Ch. 2.

Herrick, T.H. *Bank Analysts' Handbook*, New York: John Wiley and Sons, 1978.

Johnson, F., and R. Johnson. *Commercial Bank Management*, Chicago: The Dryden Press, 1985, Chs. 4 and 15.

Koch, T. W. *Bank Management*, Chicago: Dryden Press, 1988.

Mason, J. *Financial Management of Commercial Banks*, Boston: Warren, Gorham, and Lamont, 1979.

Office of the Comptroller of the Currency. *Bank Failure: An Evaluation of the Factors Contributing to the Failure of National Banks*, Washington, D.C., June 1988.

Patten, J. *Fundamentals of Bank Accounting*, Reston, Virginia: Reston Publishing Co., 1983.

Reed, E., and E. Gill. *Commercial Banking*, Fourth Edition, Englewood Cliffs, New Jersey: Prentice-Hall, Inc., 1989, Ch. 8.

Rose, P. *The Changing Structure of American Banking*, New York: Columbia University Press, 1987, Part II.

Rose, P., and D. Fraser. *Financial Institutions*, 3rd Edition, Dallas: Business Publications, Inc., 1988, Ch. 8.

Sinkey, J. *Commercial Bank Financial Management in the Financial Services Industry*, Second Edition, New York: MacMillan Publishing Co., 1986, Ch. 7.

Sinkey, J. *Problem and Failed Institutions in the Commercial Banking Industry*, Greenwich, Connecticut: JAI Press, 1979.

Wood, O., and R. Porter. *Analysis of Bank Financial Statements*, New York: Van Nostrand Reinhold Company, 1979.

Yeager, F., and N. Seitz. *Financial Institution Management*, 3rd Edition, Englewood Cliffs, New Jersey: Prentice-Hall, 1989, Ch. 6.

B. Articles

Amel, D., and M. Jacowski. "Trends in Banking Structure Since the Mid 1970s," *Federal Reserve Bulletin*, (March 1989)

Baer, H., and L. Mote. "The Effects of Nationwide Banking on Concentration - Evidence From Abroad," *Federal Reserve Bank of Chicago Economic Perspectives*, (January/February 1985)

Barth, J., R. Brumbaugh, D. Sauerhaft, and G. Wang. "Thrift Institution Failures: Causes and Policy Issues," *Proceedings of a Conference on Bank Structure and Competition*, Federal Reserve Bank of Chicago, (May 1-3, 1985): 184-216.

Booker, I. "Management Errors Litter the Steps to the Closed Doors of '82," *ABA Banking Journal*, (July 1983): 31-41.

Bovenzi, J., J. Marino, and F. McFadden. "Commercial Bank Failure Prediction Models," *Federal Reserve Bank of Atlanta Economic Review*, (November 1983): 14-26.

Bovenzi, J., and L. Nejezchleb. "Bank Failures: Why Are There So Many?" *Issues in Bank Regulation*, (Winter 1985): 54-67.

Bovenzi, J., and A. Morton. "Resolution Costs of Bank Failures," *FDIC Banking Review*, (Fall 1988)

Cates, D. "Bank Risk and Predicting Bank Failure," *Issues in Bank Regulation*, (Autumn 1985): 13-24.

Cates, D. "Management Discipline: The True Bulwark Against Banking Crisis," *Issues in Bank Regulation*, (Winter 1985): 4-10.

Clair, R. "Financial Strategies of Top-Planning Banks in the Eleventh District," *Federal Reserve Bank of Dallas Review*, (January 1987): 1-13.

Cole, D. "A Return-on-Equity Model for Banks," *The Bankers Magazine*, (Summer 1987): 40-47.

Cole, R., and A. Cornyn. "Using the Equilibrium Capital Ratio for Analysis," *Magazine of Bank Administration*, (February 1982): 46-49.

Felgram, S. "Interest Rate Swaps: Use, Risk, and Prices," *Federal Reserve Bank of Boston, New England Economic Review*, (November/December 1987): 22-32.

Gillis, H., N. Lumry, W. Rufus, and T. Oswald. "A New Approach to Analyzing Bank Performance," *The Bankers Magazine*, (March/April 1980): 67-73.

Holt, R., and K. Walewski, "Consistent High Performance Banks, 1978–1982," *The Magazine of Bank Administration*, (April 1984): 75-78.

James, C. "Off-Balance Sheet Banking," *Federal Reserve Bank of San Francisco Economic Review*, (Fall 1987): 21-36.

Kaufman, G. "Banking Risks in Historical Perspective," *Proceedings of a Conference on Bank Structure and Competition, Federal Reserve Bank of Chicago*, (May 14-16, 1986): 231-249.

Keeton, W., and C. Morris. "Why Do Banks' Loan Losses Differ?" *Federal Reserve Bank of Kansas City Economic Review*, (May 1987): 3-21.

Korobow, L., D. Stuhr, and D. Martin. "A Nationwide Test of Early Warning Research in Banking," *Federal Reserve Bank of New York Quarterly Review*, (Autumn 1977): 37-52.

Lawrence, E., D. Kummer and N. Arshadi, "Insider Borrowing Practices of Commercial Banks," *Issues in Bank Regulation*, (Summer 1987): 28-32.

Martin, D. "Early Warnings of Bank Failure: A Logit Regression Approach," *Journal of Banking and Finance*, (November 1977): 249-277.

Pantalone, C., and M. Platt. "Predicting Commercial Bank Failure Since Deregulation," *Federal Reserve Bank of Boston New England Economic Review*, (July/August 1987): 37-47.

Parker, G. "The Levers of Bank Performance," *The Bankers Magazine*, (November/December 1983): 24-30.

Peterson, R., and W. Scott. "Major Cause of Bank Failures," in *Proceedings of a Conference on Bank Structure and Competition*, Federal Reserve Bank of Chicago, (May 1-5, 1985): 166-183.

Pettway, R. "The Effects of Large Bank Failure Upon Investor's Risk Cognizance in the Commercial Banking Industry," *Journal of Financial and Quantitative Analysis*, (September 1976): 465-477.

Putnam, B. "Early Warning Systems and Financial Analysis in Bank Monitoring," *Federal Reserve Bank of Atlanta Economic Review*, (November 1983): 6-12.

Randall, Richard E., "Can The Market Evaluate Asset Quality Exposure in Banks,?" *Federal Reserve Bank of Boston New England Economic Review*, (July-August 1989): 3–24

Ricketts, D., and R. Stover. "An Examination of Bank Financial Ratios," *Journal of Bank Research*, (Summer 1978): 121-124.

Robinson, R. "Toward Improved Analysis of Bank Management," *The Bankers Magazine,* (September/October 1980): 82-87.

Rose, P., and W. Scott. "Risk in Commercial Banking: Evidence from Postwar Failures," *Southern Economic Journal,* (July 1979): 90-106.

Schick, R., and L. Sherman. "Bank Stock Prices as an Early Warning System for Changes in Condition," *Journal of Bank Research,* (Autumn 1980): 136-146.

Shaffer, S. "Challenges to Small Bank Survival," *Federal Reserve Bank of Philadelphia Business Review,* (September-October 1989): 15-27.

Short, E., G. O'Driscoll, and F. Berger. "Recent Bank Failures: Determinants and Consequences," Paper presented at the 1985 Conference on Bank Structure and Competition, Federal Reserve Bank of Chicago, (May 1-3, 1985).

Simpson, W. "Capital Market Prediction of Large Commercial Bank Failures: An Alternative Analysis," *The Financial Review,* (February 1983): 33-55.

Sinkey, J. "Risk Regulation in the Banking Industry," *Proceedings of the 1984 Conference on Bank Structure and Competition,* Federal Reserve Bank of Chicago, (May 1984): 452-460.

Sinkey, J. "A Multivariate Statistical Analysis of the Characteristics of Problem Banks," *The Journal of Finance,* (March 1975): 21-38.

Sinkey, J. "The Characteristics of Large Problem and Failed Banks," *Issues in Bank Regulation,* (Winter 1985): 43-53.

Sinkey, J., J. Terza, and R. Dince. "A Zeta Analysis of Failed Commercial Banks," *Quarterly Journal of Business and Economics*, (Autumn 1987): 35-49.

Stover, R., and J. Miller. "Additional Evidence on the Capital Market Effects of Bank Failures," *Financial Management*, (Spring 1983): 36-41.

Stuhr, D., and R. Van Wicklen. "Rating the Financial Condition of Banks: A Statistical Analysis to Aid Bank Supervision," *Federal Reserve Bank of New York Monthly Review*, (September 1974): 233-238.

Turner, W. "A Better Way to Measure Retail Banking Performance," *The Bankers Magazine*, (November/December 1978): 69-75.

Wall, L. "Why Are Some Banks More Profitable?" *Federal Reserve Bank of Atlanta Economic Review*, (September 1983): 42-48.

Watro, P. "Bank Earnings: Comparing the Extremes," *Federal Reserve Bank of Cleveland Economic Commentary*, (November 15, 1985): 1-4.

Watro, P. "Have the Characteristics of High-Earning Banks Changed? Evidence from Ohio," *Federal Reserve Bank of Cleveland Economic Commentary*, (September 1, 1989): 1-4.

West, R. "A Factor-Analytic Approach to Bank Condition," *Journal of Banking and Finance*, (June 1985): 253-266.

Whalen, G., and R. Schweitzer. "Bank Size and Risk: A Note on the Evidence," *Federal Reserve Bank of Atlanta Economic Review*, (November 1982): 32-34.

173